INTERNATIONAL CRIMINAL COURT: POLICY, STATUS AND OVERVIEW

INTERNATIONAL CRIMINAL COURT: POLICY, STATUS AND OVERVIEW

HARRY P. MILTON

EDITOR

Nova Science Publishers, Inc.

New York

LIBRARY OF CONGRESS CATALOGING-IN-PUBLICATION DATA

ISBN: 978-1-60692-723-6

Published by Nova Science Publishers, Inc. ;
New York

CONTENTS

PREFACE

Chapter 1 - The International Criminal Court (ICC), which was established in 2002, has to- date initiated investigations exclusively in Sub-Saharan Africa. The ICC Prosecutor has opened cases against 12 individuals for alleged crimes in northern Uganda, the Democratic Republic of Congo, the Central African Republic, and the Darfur region of Sudan. In addition, the Prosecutor is analyzing situations — a preliminary step toward initiating a full investigation — in Côte d'Ivoire, Kenya, and Chad, as well as in Colombia, Afghanistan, and Georgia. Recent congressional interest in the work of the ICC in Africa has arisen from concern over gross human rights violations on the continent. Legislation before the 110th Congress references the ICC with respect to several ongoing African conflicts, including those in northern Uganda, the Democratic Republic of Congo, and the Darfur region of Sudan.

On July 14, 2008, the ICC Prosecutor requested a warrant for the arrest of Sudanese President Omar Hassan al-Bashir, accusing him of genocide, crimes against humanity, and war crimes in Darfur. The request, which awaits a decision by a panel of ICC judges, represents the first attempt by the ICC to prosecute a sitting head of state, and the first ICC case to cite the crime of genocide. Although the Prosecutor's action has drawn praise from human rights advocates, it also has raised fears that ICC actions in Sudan could threaten ongoing peace processes in Darfur and southern Sudan or endanger international humanitarian and peacekeeping operations. Unlike the three other African countries under ICC investigation, Sudan is not a party to the ICC. Instead, the ICC was granted jurisdiction over Darfur through a United Nations Security Council resolution in March 2005. The United States, as a member of the Security Council, can influence the ICC's actions. The Bush Administration, which holds the Sudanese government responsible for genocide, has sought to balance its strong opposition to the ICC with its policy on alleged crimes in Darfur.

Four suspects in other ICC investigations are currently in ICC custody, pending trial. Three are alleged leaders of Congolese militias, and the fourth is a former Congolese vice president, senator, and former rebel leader who is accused of crimes committed in neighboring Central African Republic. This report provides background on ICC investigations in Africa and gives an overview of cases currently before the Court. The report also examines issues raised by the ICC's actions in Africa, including the ICC's possible role in deterring future abuses and the potential impact of international criminal prosecutions on peace processes, ongoing in many countries on the continent.

In-depth background on U.S. policy toward the ICC can be found in CRS Report RL3 1495, *U.S. Policy Regarding the International Criminal Court*, by Jennifer K. Elsea. Further background on Sudan and an analysis of U.S. policy options can be found in CRS Report RL3 3574, *Sudan: The Crisis in Darfur and Status of the North- South Peace Agreement*, by Ted Dagne. This report may be updated as events warrant.

Chapter 2 - One month after the International Criminal Court (ICC) officially came into existence on July 1, 2002, the President signed the American Servicemembers' Protection Act (ASPA), which limits U.S. government support and assistance to the ICC; curtails certain military assistance to many countries that have ratified the Rome Statute establishing the ICC; regulates U.S. participation in United Nations (U.N.) peacekeeping missions commenced after July 1, 2003; and, most controversially among European allies, authorizes the President to use "all means necessary and appropriate to bring about the release" of certain U.S. and allied persons who may be detained or tried by the ICC. The provision withholding military assistance under the programs for Foreign Military Financing (FMF) and International Military Education and Training (IMET) from certain States Parties to the Rome Statute came into effect on July 1, 2003. The 1 09th Congress reauthorized the Nethercutt Amendment as part of the FY2006 Consolidated Appropriations Act (H.R. 3057/P.L. 109-102). Unless waived by the President, it bars Economic Support Funds (ESF) assistance to countries that have not agreed to protect U.S. citizens from being turned over to the ICC for prosecution. H.R. 5522, as passed by the House of Representatives, would continue the ESF restriction for FY2007. The Senate passed a measure as part of the 2007 National Defense Authorization Act (H.R. 5122, S. 2766) that would modify ASPA to end the ban on IMET assistance.

The ICC is the first permanent world court with nearly universal jurisdiction to try individuals accused of war crimes, crimes against humanity, genocide, and possibly aggression. While most U.S. allies support the ICC, the Bush

Administration firmly opposes it and has renounced any U.S. obligations under the treaty. After the Bush Administration threatened to veto a United Nations Security Council resolution to extend the peacekeeping mission in Bosnia on the ground that it did not contain sufficient guarantees that U.S. participants would be immune to prosecution by the ICC, the Security Council adopted a resolution that would defer for one year any prosecution of participants in missions established or authorized by the U.N. whose home countries have not ratified the Rome Statute. That resolution was renewed through July 1, 2004, but was not subsequently renewed. In addition, the United States is pursuing bilateral "Article 98"agreements to preclude extradition by other countries of U.S. citizens to the ICC. However, in what some view as a sign that the Administration is softening its stance with respect to the ICC, the United States did not exercise its veto power at the Security Council to prevent the referral of a case against Sudan's leaders for the alleged genocide in Darfur.

This report outlines the main objections the United States has raised with respect to the ICC and analyzes ASPA and other relevant legislation enacted or proposed to regulate U.S. cooperation with the ICC. The report concludes with a discussion of the implications for the United States, as a non-ratifying country, as the ICC begins to take shape, as well as the Administration's efforts to win immunity from the ICC's jurisdiction for Americans. A description of the ICC's background and a more detailed analysis of the ICC organization, jurisdiction, and procedural rules may be found in CRS Report RL3 1437, *International Criminal Court: Overview and Selected Legal Issues*, by Jennifer K. Elsea.

Chapter 3 - The International Criminal Court (ICC) is the first global permanent international court with jurisdiction to prosecute individuals for "the most serious crimes of concern to the international community." The United Nations, many human rights organizations, and most democratic nations have expressed support for the new court. The Bush Administration firmly opposes it and has formally renounced the U.S. obligations under the treaty. At the same time, however, the Administration has stressed that the United States shares the goals of the ICC's supporters-promotion of the rule of law-and does not intend to take any action to undermine the ICC.

The primary objection given by the U.S. in opposition to the treaty is the ICC's possible assertion of the jurisdiction over U.S. soldiers charged with "war crimes" resulting from legitimate uses of force. The main issue faced by the current Congress is whether to adopt a policy aimed at preventing the ICC from becoming effective or whether to continue contributing to the development of the ICC in order to improve it.

This book provides a historical background of the negotiations for the Rome Statute, outlines the structure of the International Criminal Court (ICC) as contained in the final Statute, and describes the jurisdiction of the ICC. The book further identifies the specific crimes enumerated in the Rome Statute as supplemented by the draft elements of crime. A discussion of procedural safeguards follows, including reference to the draft procedural rules.

The book then goes on to discuss the implications for the United States as a non-ratifying country when the ICC comes into being, and outlines some legislation enacted and proposed to regulate U.S relations with the ICC.

In: International Criminal Court
Editor: Harry P. Milton, pp. 1-39

ISBN: 978-1-60692-723-6
© 2009 Nova Science Publishers, Inc.

Chapter 1

INTERNATIONAL CRIMINAL COURT CASES IN AFRICA: STATUS AND POLICY ISSUES[*]

Alexis Arieff[1], Rhoda Margesson[2]
and Marjorie Ann Browne[3]
[1] Analyst in African Affairs
Foreign Affairs, Defense, and Trade Division
[2] Specialist in International Humanitarian Policy
Foreign Affairs, Defense, and Trade Division
[3] Specialist in International Relations
Foreign Affairs, Defense, and Trade Division

ABSTRACT

The International Criminal Court (ICC), which was established in 2002, has to- date initiated investigations exclusively in Sub-Saharan Africa. The ICC Prosecutor has opened cases against 12 individuals for alleged crimes in northern Uganda, the Democratic Republic of Congo, the Central African Republic, and the Darfur region of Sudan. In addition, the Prosecutor is analyzing situations — a preliminary step toward initiating a full investigation — in Côte d'Ivoire, Kenya, and Chad, as well as in Colombia, Afghanistan, and Georgia. Recent congressional interest in the work of the ICC in Africa has arisen from concern over gross human rights violations on the continent. Legislation before the 110th Congress references the ICC with

---

[*] Excerpted from CRS Report RL34665, dated September 12, 2008.

respect to several ongoing African conflicts, including those in northern Uganda, the Democratic Republic of Congo, and the Darfur region of Sudan.

On July 14, 2008, the ICC Prosecutor requested a warrant for the arrest of Sudanese President Omar Hassan al-Bashir, accusing him of genocide, crimes against humanity, and war crimes in Darfur. The request, which awaits a decision by a panel of ICC judges, represents the first attempt by the ICC to prosecute a sitting head of state, and the first ICC case to cite the crime of genocide. Although the Prosecutor's action has drawn praise from human rights advocates, it also has raised fears that ICC actions in Sudan could threaten ongoing peace processes in Darfur and southern Sudan or endanger international humanitarian and peacekeeping operations. Unlike the three other African countries under ICC investigation, Sudan is not a party to the ICC. Instead, the ICC was granted jurisdiction over Darfur through a United Nations Security Council resolution in March 2005. The United States, as a member of the Security Council, can influence the ICC's actions. The Bush Administration, which holds the Sudanese government responsible for genocide, has sought to balance its strong opposition to the ICC with its policy on alleged crimes in Darfur.

Four suspects in other ICC investigations are currently in ICC custody, pending trial. Three are alleged leaders of Congolese militias, and the fourth is a former Congolese vice president, senator, and former rebel leader who is accused of crimes committed in neighboring Central African Republic. This report provides background on ICC investigations in Africa and gives an overview of cases currently before the Court. The report also examines issues raised by the ICC's actions in Africa, including the ICC's possible role in deterring future abuses and the potential impact of international criminal prosecutions on peace processes, ongoing in many countries on the continent.

In-depth background on U.S. policy toward the ICC can be found in CRS Report RL3 1495, *U.S. Policy Regarding the International Criminal Court*, by Jennifer K. Elsea. Further background on Sudan and an analysis of U.S. policy options can be found in CRS Report RL3 3574, *Sudan: The Crisis in Darfur and Status of the North- South Peace Agreement*, by Ted Dagne. This report may be updated as events warrant.

INTRODUCTION

The International Criminal Court (ICC) has to-date initiated investigations exclusively in Sub-Saharan Africa. Recent congressional interest in the work of the ICC in Africa has focused on the role that the ICC may play in addressing gross human rights violations on the continent. While many Members of Congress remain opposed to the Court, several pieces of legislation before the 110th Congress reference the ICC with respect to ongoing African conflicts, including those in northern Uganda, the Democratic Republic of Congo, and the Darfur region of Sudan.

Congress and the Bush Administration have each stated that genocide is occurring in Darfur.[1] On July 14, 2008, the ICC Prosecutor requested a warrant for the arrest of Sudanese President Omar Hassan al-Bashir for genocide, crimes against humanity, and war crimes in the Darfur region of Sudan. This represents the first time the ICC Prosecutor has named a sitting head of state, and the first time he has accused a suspect of genocide. While the attempt to prosecute of the Sudanese president has drawn praise from human rights advocates, the European Union, and others, it also has raised concerns that ICC actions in Sudan could threaten ongoing peace processes in Darfur and southern Sudan or endanger international humanitarian and peacekeeping operations.

This report provides background on ICC investigations in Africa and gives an overview of cases before the Court. The report also examines issues raised by the ICC's actions in Africa, including the ICC's possible role in deterring future abuses and the potential effect of international criminal prosecutions on peace processes.

BACKGROUND

Overview of the International Criminal Court

The Statute of the ICC, also known as the Rome Statute, entered into force on July 1, 2002, and established a permanent, independent Court to investigate and bring to justice individuals who commit the most heinous violations of international law and human rights, namely war crimes, crimes against humanity, and genocide.[2] The ICC's jurisdiction extends only over crimes committed since the entry into force of the Statute. The ICC is headquartered in The Hague, Netherlands. As of June 1, 2008, 106 countries were parties to the Statute.[3] The United States is not a party to the ICC. The Assembly of States Parties (the body made up of the 106 parties) provides administrative oversight and other support for the Court, including adoption of the budget and election of 18 judges, the Prosecutor (currently Luis Moreno-Ocampo from Argentina), and the Registrar (currently Bruno Cathala from France).[4]

Situations[5] may be referred to the ICC in one of three ways as outlined in the articles of the Statute: by a state party to the Statute, the ICC Prosecutor, or the United Nations (U.N.) Security Council. Currently, four situations have been publicly referred to the Prosecutor. The governments of three countries (all parties to the ICC) — Uganda, the Democratic Republic of Congo, and the Central African

Republic — each have referred situations to the Prosecutor. The U.N. Security Council has referred one situation (Darfur, Sudan) to the Prosecutor.[6] At least two potential situations were dismissed following preliminary analysis, and at least six others remain under consideration.[7]

The ICC is considered a court of last resort — it will only investigate or prosecute cases of the most serious crimes perpetrated by individuals (not organizations or governments), and then, only when national judicial systems are unwilling or unable to handle them. This principle of admissibility before the Court is known as "complementarity."[8] Although many domestic legal systems grant sitting heads of state immunity from criminal prosecution, the Rome Statute grants the ICC jurisdiction over any individual, regardless of official capacity.[9]

The U.S. Position on the ICC

The United States is not a party to the Rome Statute. The Bush Administration firmly opposes the Court and has renounced any U.S. obligations under the treaty.[10] It objects to the Court on a number of grounds, including:

- the Court's assertion of jurisdiction (in certain circumstances) over citizens, including military personnel, of countries that are not parties to the treaty[11];
- the perceived lack of adequate checks and balances on the powers of the ICC prosecutors and judges;
- the perceived dilution of the role of the U.N. Security Council in maintaining peace and security; and
- the ICC's potentially chilling effect on America's willingness to project power in the defense of its interests.

The Administration has sought to conclude bilateral immunity agreements (BIAs), known as "Article 98 agreements," with most states parties to exempt U.S. citizens from possible surrender to the ICC.[12] These agreements are named for Article 98(2) of the Statute, which bars the ICC from asking for surrender of persons from a state party that would require it to act contrary to its international obligations.

The U.S. government is prohibited by law from assisting the ICC in its investigations, arrests, detentions, extraditions, or prosecutions of war crimes, under the American Servicemembers' Protection Act of 2002, or ASPA (P.L. 107-206, Title II). The prohibition is extensive, covering, among other things, the obligation of appropriated funds, assistance in investigations on U.S. territory, participation in U.N. peacekeeping operations unless certain protections from ICC actions are provided to specific categories of people, and the sharing of classified and law enforcement information.[13]

The ICC and Other International Courts and Tribunals

The post- World War II Nuremberg and Tokyo tribunals to prosecute Nazi and Japanese leaders for crimes against peace, war crimes, and crimes against humanity established precedent for the ICC. Other international courts and tribunals, such as the International Criminal Tribunals for the former Yugoslavia and for Rwanda, also built on these precedents. However, there are some important distinctions between the work of the ICC and that of courts created with limited jurisdiction. The ICC was established through a multilateral treaty and is a permanent, international criminal tribunal.[14] It is not a U.N. body. By contrast, the tribunals for the former Yugoslavia[15] and Rwanda,[16] which were created under separate U.N. Security Council resolutions to address the allegations of crimes against humanity in those countries, are case specific, limited in jurisdiction, and temporary. The Security Council may establish international criminal tribunals on a case-by-case basis.

Numerous regional and other international courts and tribunals also have been created, some on an *ad hoc* basis, to address particular issues.[17] For example, there are options for mixed courts, which may consist of both international judges and prosecutors as well as judges and prosecutors having the nationality of the state in which the trial takes place. Moreover, a mixed court may draw on domestic as well as international law. The mixed court may be part of the judicial organ of the state, as in Kosovo, Cambodia, or Timor-Leste, or it may be more international in the form of a special court, such as the one established for Sierra Leone.[18] These courts and tribunals are distinct from the ICC.

International Court of Justice

The International Court of Justice (ICJ), also located in The Hague, is the principal judicial organ of the United Nations. The ICJ does not prosecute individuals; its role is to settle, in accordance with international law, legal disputes submitted to it by states. Only states may submit cases for consideration, although the ICJ also will give advisory opinions on legal questions when requested to do so by authorized international organizations.[19]

Congressional Interest in the ICC in Africa

Members of Congress have taken a range of positions on the ICC with regard to Africa. On the one hand, many in Congress are concerned about massive human rights violations on the continent, and some see the ICC as a possible means of redress for these crimes. On the other hand, many oppose• the ICC on jurisdictional grounds. Congressional support remains for some restrictions on U.S. assistance to countries that are parties to the ICC and that have not signed bilateral immunity agreements with the United States. However, restrictions on military assistance to ICC members under the American Servicemembers' Protection Act of 2002, or ASPA (P.L. 107-206, Title II), were repealed under the National Defense Authorization Acts for FY2007 and FY2008. Overall, a combination of presidential waivers and changes to the law have effectively nullified restrictions on U.S. assistance to African parties to the ICC.

Atrocities in African Conflicts

There has been particular congressional interest in the ICC's work related to Darfur. Recent legislation also has referenced the ICC in connection with ongoing conflicts in Uganda and the Democratic Republic of Congo. . Examples during the 110th Congress include

- H.R. 6416, *The Just and Lasting Peace in Sudan Act of 2008*, introduced on June 26, 2008, which would make Sudanese compliance with ICC arrest warrants a condition for lifting existing sanctions on Sudan (referred to the House Committee on Foreign Affairs);
- H.Res. 1227, *Condemning sexual violence in the Democratic Republic of the Congo and calling on the international community to take immediate actions to respond to the violence*, introduced on May 22, 2008 (referred to the House Committee on Foreign Affairs);
- H.R. 180, *The Darfur Accountability and Divestment Act of 2007*, which would offer U.S. support to the ICC's efforts to prosecute those responsible for acts of genocide in Darfur, passed by the House on August 3, 2007 (referred to the Senate Committee on Banking, Housing, and Urban Affairs);
- H.Con.Res. 80, *Calling on the Government of Uganda and the Lord's Resistance Army (LRA) to recommit to a political solution to the conflict in northern Uganda by engaging in good-faith negotiations*, passed by the House on June 19, 2007 (referred to the Senate Committee on Foreign Relations).

Restrictions on U.S. Assistance to African Parties to the ICC

Observers have raised concerns over the possible assertion of ICC jurisdiction over U.S. military personnel in connection with U.S. participation in U.N. peacekeeping missions in Africa, and with respect to the new U.S. Combatant Command for Africa, AFRICOM.[20] Jurisdictional and other concerns led Congress to pass the American Servicemembers' Protection Act of 2002, or ASPA (P.L. 107-206, Title II), which was signed into law on August 2, 2002. Section 2007 of ASPA prohibited U.S. military assistance to ICC member-states, except for NATO countries, major non-NATO allies, and countries subject to various other waiver provisions. Permanent waivers were granted to countries that ratified Article 98 agreements promising not to surrender U.S. nationals to the Court.

In Sub-Saharan Africa, ASPA effectively froze International Military Education and Training (IMET), Foreign Military Financing (FMF), and Excess Defense Articles (EDA) accounts for Kenya, Mali, Namibia, Niger, South Africa, and Tanzania. However, President Bush waived the prohibition on IMET assistance to 21 countries, including these six, on September 29, 2006, due to concerns that the restrictions could preclude valuable military-to-military ties.[21] Congress repealed the ASPA restriction on IMET funding in the National Defense Authorization Act for FY2007 (P.L. 109-364), which was signed into law on October 17, 2006. The National Defense Authorization Act for FY2008 (P.L. 110-181), signed into law on January 28, 2008, repealed Section 2007 of ASPA entirely, ending remaining prohibitions on FMF and EDA assistance.

Separately, the Nethercutt Amendment to the FY2005 Consolidated Appropriations Act (P.L. 108-447), signed into law December 8, 2004, prohibited Economic Support Fund (ESF) assistance to members of the ICC that had not entered into an Article 98 agreement with the United States, with certain waiver provisions. This prohibition was included as part of the FY2006 Consolidated Appropriations Act (P.L. 109-102, Section 574), which was signed into law on November 14, 2005. The prohibition was subsequently carried over via continuing resolutions on February 15, 2007 (P.L. 110-5) and September 29, 2007 (P.L. 110-92). A substantially identical restriction was included in the Consolidated Appropriations Act of 2008 (P.L. 110-161, Section 671), signed into law December 26, 2007. President Bush has twice waived this restriction with respect to 14 countries, including, in Africa, Kenya, Mali, Namibia, Niger, South Africa, and Tanzania.[22]

THE ICC AND SUDAN

Sudan is a unique case because of the circumstances of ICC involvement, and because of whom the ICC Prosecutor has chosen to pursue. ICC jurisdiction in Sudan was referred by the U.N. Security Council, as Sudan is not a party to the Court. In September 2004, the Security Council established an International Commission of Inquiry on Darfur under Resolution 1564, citing concern that the Sudanese government had not met its obligations under previous Resolutions.[23] In January 2005, the Commission reported that it had compiled a confidential list of potential war crimes suspects, and "strongly recommend[ed]" that the Security Council refer the situation in Darfur to the ICC.[24] On March 31, 2005, U.N. Security Council Resolution 1593 referred the situation in Darfur to the ICC Prosecutor. Following the referral, the ICC Prosecutor received the document archive of the Commission of Inquiry. The Office of the Prosecutor initiated its own investigation in June 2005.

In May 2007, the ICC issued arrest warrants for a former Sudanese Cabinet Minister and an alleged former leader of the Janjaweed militia in Darfur. The Sudanese government has refused to comply with the warrants, and both suspects remain at large. The Prosecutor is also investigating alleged attacks on peacekeepers by rebels in Darfur.

On July 14, 2008, the ICC Prosecutor applied for a warrant for the arrest of Sudanese President Omar Hassan al-Bashir for genocide, crimes against humanity, and war crimes. The application for a warrant is the first time the ICC Prosecutor has named a sitting head of state, and the first time he has accused a suspect of genocide. The request has provoked condemnation in Sudan and controversy in the region. Several African and Middle Eastern governments and regional organizations have called for a U.N. Security Council deferral of the prosecution in the interest of peace and security. This section concludes with an analysis of Security Council deliberations in July 2008, including discussion of a possible deferral under Article 16 of the ICC Statute.

U.N. Security Council Resolution 1593

On March 31, 2005, the U.N. Security Council, acting under Chapter VII of the U.N. Charter, adopted Resolution 1593 (2005), which refers reports about the situation in Darfur, Sudan (dating back to July 1, 2002) to the ICC Prosecutor.[25] The Resolution was adopted by a vote of 11 in favor, none against, and with four abstentions — the United States, China, Algeria, and Brazil.[26] While

Sudan is not a party to the ICC and has not consented to its jurisdiction, the case can be referred to the ICC by the U.N. Security Council under Chapter VII. The Resolution is binding on all U.N. member states, including Sudan. Under the ICC Statute, the ICC is authorized, but not required, to accept the case.[27]

The U.S. Position on U.N. Security Council Resolution 1593

In statements made in July and September 2004, respectively, Congress and the Bush Administration declared that genocide was taking place in Darfur. The Administration supported the formation of the International Commission of Inquiry for Darfur.[28] However, the Bush Administration preferred a special tribunal in Africa to be the mechanism of accountability for those who committed crimes in Darfur. It objected to the U.N. Security Council referral to the ICC because of its stated objections to the ICC's jurisdiction over nationals of states not party to the Rome Statute.[29] However, the United States had supported a version of the Rome Statute that would have allowed the U.N. Security Council to refer cases involving non- states parties to the ICC, but would not have allowed other states or the Prosecutor to refer cases. The United States abstained on Resolution 1593 (which is not equivalent to a veto in the Security Council) because the Resolution included language that dealt with the sovereignty questions of concern and essentially protected U.S. nationals and other persons of non-party States other than Sudan from prosecution.[30] The abstention did not change the fundamental objections of the Bush Administration to the ICC.

At the same time, the Bush Administration has supported the need for the international community to come together and take action on the atrocities occurring in Darfur.[31] The Administration and Congress have expressed support for bringing to justice those who perpetrate genocide, war crimes, and crimes against humanity in the region. However, U.S. legal restrictions on providing assistance to the ICC present an obstacle to the use of the ICC for that purpose.

ICC Warrants

In May 2007, the ICC issued arrest warrants for Ahmad Muhammad Harun, who had served as Interior Minister from 2003 and 2005, and Ali Muhammad Ali Abd-Al-Rahman (known as Ali Kushayb), who had allegedly acted as leader of the Janjaweed in the Wadi Salih area of Darfur.[32] They were each accused of over 40 counts of war crimes and crimes against humanity in connection with abuses allegedly committed in Darfur in 2003 and 2004.[33]

The Sudanese government has refused to comply with the ICC warrants, and neither suspect is in ICC custody. Reports suggest Kushayb was in Sudanese detention when the arrest warrant was issued, but has since been released, while Harun was promoted to Minister of Humanitarian Affairs and co-president of a committee to investigate human rights violations in Sudan.[34] In 2005, following the initiation of the ICC's investigation, the Sudanese government created its own special courts for Darfur in an apparent effort to stave off the ICC's jurisdiction under the principle of complementarity. However, the courts' efforts were widely criticized as insufficient.[35] They have reportedly been largely dormant since 2007.[36]

Investigation of Rebel Crimes

In December 2007, the ICC Prosecutor announced the opening of a new investigation into the targeting of peacekeepers and aid workers in Darfur. In June 2008, the Prosecutor stated that the investigation was focusing on the September 29, 2007, attack on the town of Haskanita in which ten peacekeepers — then serving under the African Union Mission in Sudan (AMIS) — were killed. The Prosecutor said the Haskanita attack appeared to have been committed by rebel forces, but he has not yet named the accused.[37]

The Case Against Bashir

Application for a Warrant

On July 14, 2008, ICC Prosecutor Moreno-Ocampo applied for a warrant for the arrest of Sudanese President Omar Hassan al-B ashir.[38] The application presented evidence implicating Bashir in three counts of genocide, five counts of crimes against humanity, and two counts of war crimes.[39] The accusations refer to alleged attacks by Sudanese troops and pro-government militias against civilians in the Darfur region of Sudan during the government's five-year counter-insurgency campaign. Moreno-Ocampo affirmed that while Bashir did not "physically or directly" carry out abuses, "he committed these crimes through members of the state apparatus, the army, and the Militia/Janjaweed" as president and commander-in-chief of the armed forces.[40] Although many domestic legal systems grant sitting heads of state immunity from criminal prosecution, the Rome Statute grants the ICC jurisdiction over any individual, regardless of official capacity.[41]

The application for a warrant is not an indictment; under ICC procedures, charges must be confirmed at a pre-trial hearing. Having received the application, a panel of ICC judges known as the Pre-Trial Chamber must decide whether to issue a warrant for Bashir's arrest. The decision is expected to take into account whether there are "reasonable grounds" to believe Bashir committed the alleged crimes, and whether a warrant is necessary to ensure Bashir's appearance in court. In response to the request for a warrant, several European governments, including France and Great Britain, have called on the Sudanese government to comply with ICC actions. Reactions by regional governments have been more critical, with many calling for a deferral of the prosecution. The governments of Russia and China have voiced opposition to the prosecution attempt. An analysis in the *Chicago Tribune* noted that if a warrant is issued, "Sudan is unlikely to hand over the president, but the warrant would mean that Bashir could be arrested by international authorities if he left his country."[42]

Genocide[43]

Bashir is the first individual to be accused of genocide by the ICC Prosecutor. The request for a warrant alleges that Bashir "intends to destroy in substantial part the Fur, Masalit and Zaghawa ethnic groups as such" through coordinated attacks by government troops and Janjaweed militia members on civilian targets, including villages, towns, and camps for internally displaced persons.[44] The prosecution's case states that 35,000 people in Darfur have been killed outright, at least 2,700,000 displaced, and thousands raped in such attacks, and that most victims are members of the targeted groups.[45] The case is based on the Prosecutor's own investigation, which was initiated in June 2005, as well as on thousands of documents, video footage, and interview transcripts received from the U.N. International Commission of Inquiry on Darfur. The Prosecutor also received the Commission's sealed list of individuals suspected of committing serious abuses in Darfur, though this list is not binding on the selection of suspects.

Human rights organizations and Darfur advocacy groups have welcomed the prosecution of Bashir for genocide.[46] However, the formulation of the Prosecutor's accusation has drawn some criticism. The Commission of Inquiry concluded in its January 2005 report that the violence in Darfur did not amount to genocide, but that "international offences such as the crimes against humanity and war crimes that have been committed in Darfur may be no less serious and heinous than genocide."[47] Many Darfur activists have accused the Commission of allowing political considerations to affect its conclusions.[48] Other analysts, such as the scholar Alex de Waal, argue that while the Sudanese government is responsible for serious crimes in Darfur, the charge of genocide will be "extraordinarily difficult" to prove.[49]

Sudanese Reactions

The Sudanese government has rejected ICC jurisdiction over Darfur as a violation of its sovereignty and accused the Court of being part of a Western plot against a sovereign African and Muslim state.[50] Other reactions have focused on the potential impact of an arrest warrant on ongoing peace processes, peacekeeping operations, and humanitarian relief, and on the potential impact on national elections scheduled for 2009.

The Bashir Administration

Reports suggest that Bashir's administration sees the ICC as an instrument of Western pressure for regime change in Sudan, and not as an independent institution.[51] The Sudanese president has repeatedly denied that genocide or ethnic cleansing is taking place in Darfur and has rejected ICC jurisdiction as an infringement on Sudanese sovereignty.[52] The last mission to Sudan by ICC prosecutorial staff was in January-February 2007, after which the government announced it would no longer allow ICC personnel to speak to Sudanese officials.[53]

Days before the request for a warrant against Bashir was announced, a presidential spokesman reportedly called the Prosecutor a "terrorist" whose investigation was based on testimony by rebel leaders and spies posing as humanitarian workers.[54] The ruling National Congress Party (NCP) has used state-controlled media and public demonstrations to rally domestic support and emphasize that ICC actions are "aimed at core national values and strategic interests."[55] Shortly after the request for a warrant was announced, Bashir undertook a good-will tour to Darfur, where he reportedly promised new development initiatives for the region and was greeted by thousands of supporters. At the regional level, the Sudanese government launched a diplomatic campaign to lobby for a U.N. Security Council deferral of the case (see section below). According to press reports, in mid-August 2008, government troops launched a new offensive in northern Darfur to seize control of rebel strongholds.

In a further effort to preclude prosecution, Bashir has argued that Sudan has the capacity to investigate and try perpetrators of violence in Darfur domestically.[56] In early August 2008, the government appointed a special prosecutor, Nimer Ibrahim Mohamed, to investigate alleged crimes in Darfur. The appointment is in addition to the special courts created after ICC warrants were issued for Harun and Kushayb. While Mohamed is reportedly a respected lawyer, observers suggest that his efforts will be limited by political pressures, and that Sudanese law does not contain provisions for genocide, war crimes, or crimes against humanity.[57]

While the ICC is institutionally independent from the United Nations, Sudanese officials have reportedly on multiple occasions threatened the safety of U.N. personnel in Sudan if an arrest warrant is issued, including those serving the U.N. Mission in Sudan (UNMIS, in the South) and the African Union-United Nations Hybrid Operation in Darfur (UNAMID).[58] At the same time, at least one official denied that the government was threatening U.N. staff.[59] Seven peacekeepers were killed and 22 injured in an ambush in Darfur on July 8, 2008, deepening fears of reprisals.[60]

Other Sudanese Reactions

Some Sudanese opposition parties have displayed public support for the president, reportedly due in part to concerns that an ICC arrest warrant could derail elections scheduled for 2009, while privately acknowledging mixed reactions.[61] Spokesmen for the two largest Darfur rebel factions, the Sudan Liberation Movement-Unity (SLM-U) and the Justice and Equality Movement (JEM), have reportedly welcomed the request for a warrant against Bashir.[62]

Media reports suggest southern Sudanese are ambivalent about the attempt to prosecute Bashir[63][3] The Sudan People's Liberation Movement (SPLM) — the former southern rebel group and partner in the Government of National Unity under the 2005 Comprehensive Peace Agreement (CPA) — called on the Government of National Unity "to forge an understanding with the international community and to cooperate with [the] ICC on the legal processes."[64] The SPLM also expressed concern that the ICC's move could threaten "peace and stability" in Sudan, and affirmed that the situation in Darfur "requires a negotiated and peaceful settlement."[65] Some SPLM officials are reportedly concerned that ICC attempts to prosecute Bashir could undo the CPA, while others have reportedly expressed hope that prosecution could leverage international pressure on Khartoum.[66] Following the request for a warrant, Bashir appointed the SPLM's Salva Kiir, the President of south Sudan and first Vice President in the Government of National Unity, to head a government commission to coordinate Sudan's response to the ICC. Kiir reportedly traveled to Uganda in late July and urged the country's leadership to support a delay in the proceedings against Bashir.[67] The ruling party has averred that "the position of the SPLM... is based on full solidarity with the president," according to local media, though observers dispute this assertion.[68]

Regional Reactions

The Sudanese government has rallied support for a deferral of Bashir's potential prosecution among Arab and African leaders, as well as among regional organizations such as the African Union (AU), the Arab League, and the

Organization of the Islamic Conference (OIC).[69] In a written statement on July 11, 2008, the AU Peace and Security Council "expressed its strong conviction that the search for justice should be pursued in a way that does not impede or jeopardize efforts aimed at promoting a lasting peace" and "reiterated [the] AU's concern with the misuse of indictments against African leaders."[70] On July 21 and July 22, respectively, the AU Peace and Security Council and the OIC's Group in New York requested that the U.N. Security Council suspend ICC proceedings in the interests of peace and stability.[71] The AU also called on the Sudanese government to investigate human rights violations in Darfur, and is reportedly planning its own investigation in the region, with Sudanese cooperation.[72] The President of the AU Commission, Jean Ping, and the joint U.N.-AU mediator for Darfur, Djibril Bassolet, have raised concerns that the ICC is jeopardizing peace efforts.[73] On July 31, the Non-Aligned Movement of 120 developing countries expressed "deep concern" that the prosecution of Bashir could destabilize Sudan.[74]

Many African and Middle Eastern governments have expressed concern over the attempt to prosecute Bashir, including those of South Africa, Nigeria, Kenya, Rwanda, Tanzania, Benin, Eritrea, Egypt, Iran, Syria, Libya, Algeria, and Morocco. President Yoweri Museveni of Uganda, on the other hand, has taken a public stance in favor of ICC involvement in Darfur, a position that appears to stem in part from the ICC's prosecutions of rebel leaders in Uganda.[75] Some African and Middle Eastern commentators have praised the ICC Prosecutor's decision to pursue Bashir as an important step against impunity in the region, while others wondered whether the move displayed bias against African countries.[76]

Security Council Considerations in July 2008

The July 14, 2008, ICC Prosecutor's request for an arrest warrant for Bashir occurred during the time that the U.N. Security Council was considering extension of the Council mandate for the African Union-United Nations Hybrid Operation in Darfur (UNAMID). The Council had before it the report of the U.N. Secretary-General on the deployment of the operation, dated July 7 and covering the period April to June 2008.[77] It was expected that this mandate, which was to expire July 31, would be extended, albeit with some discussion of UNAMID-related issues.

Council considerations were significantly impacted by the ICC Prosecutor's announcement. In the light of reactions to this request (see previous section) and in view of the fact that the Council had sent the case to the ICC for investigation, protracted consultations within the Council on the content of a resolution extending the UNAMID mandate delayed Council action until nearly the final hour.[78]

Among the possible issues engaging Council members after the July 14 action was the oft-made suggestion that the Council include in its resolution a request, under Article 16 of the ICC Statute, for a deferral or suspension of further ICC action on the case for up to 12 months for the purpose of, among other things, facilitating efforts toward a peaceful settlement of the situations in Darfur and south Sudan. Some governments also expressed concerns that a positive ICC response to the request for an arrest warrant would exacerbate the situation on the ground in Darfur, making both peacekeepers and humanitarian workers subject to further attacks.

Article 16 of the ICC Statute is entitled *Deferral of investigation or prosecution* and provides that

> No investigation or prosecution can be commenced or proceeded with under this Statute for a period of 12 months after the Security Council, in a resolution adopted under Chapter VII of the Charter of the United Nations, has requested the Court to that effect; that request may be renewed by the Council under the same conditions.

Thus, if the U.N. Security Council, acting under Chapter VII of the Charter, adopts a resolution requesting the ICC to suspend or defer any further investigation or prosecution of the case against Bashir, the ICC, including the Prosecutor, would be obliged to cease its investigation in that particular situation and the Pre-Trial Chamber, before which the warrant request is pending, would have to suspend its considerations. The Council request would be applicable for 12 months and would be renewable.

David Scheffer, who headed the U.S. delegation to the conference that drafted the ICC Statute, in an August 20, 2008, Op-ed in *Jurist*, noted that the "negotiating history of Article 16 should be instructive to how the Council currently examines the Darfur situation."[79] Scheffer pointed out that Article 16 was drafted and adopted to enable the U.N. Security Council to suspend or defer an ICC investigation or prosecution of a situation *"before either is launched"* if priorities of peace and security compelled a delay of international justice." He stated that "the original intent behind Article 16 was for the Security Council to act pre-emptively to delay the application of international justice for atrocity crimes in a particular situation in order to focus exclusively on performing the Council's mandated responsibilities for international peace and security objectives." This was a tool to be employed by the Council in instances of "premature State Party or Prosecutor referrals." In addition, Scheffer observed that if the current proposals for Council suspension of further ICC action on a situation referred to the ICC by the Council had been foreseen, "Article 16 never would have been approved by the. ..majority of governments attending the U.N. talks on the Rome Statute for it would have been viewed as creating rights for the Security Council far beyond the original intent of the Singapore compromise."

Scheffer noted, "Nonetheless, one plausibly may argue that the language of Article 16 of the Rome Statute technically empowers the Security Council to intervene at this late date and block approval of an arrest warrant against President Bashir or even suspend its execution following any approval of it by the judges."[80]

U.N. Security Council Resolution 1828 (2008), adopted on July 31, 2008, by a vote of 14 in favor and with the United States abstaining, extended UNAMID for a further 12 months; the meeting, incidentally, ended at 10:45 pm.[81] In abstaining on the vote rather than voting against it, the United States supported renewal of the UNAMID mandate but noted that the language in preambular paragraph 9 "would send the wrong signal to President Bashir and undermine efforts to bring him and others to justice."[82] In remarks with the press following the vote, U.S. Deputy Permanent Representative Alejandro Wolff stated:

> The reason for our abstention.. .had to do with one paragraph that would send the wrong signal at a very important time when we are trying to eliminate the climate of impunity, to deal with justice, and to address crimes in Darfur, by suggesting that there might be a way out. There is no compromise on the issue of justice. The ... United States felt it was time to stand up on this point of moral clarity and make clear that this Permanent Member of the Security Council will not compromise on the issue of justice.[83]

OTHER ICC CASES IN AFRICA

The ICC Prosecutor has opened five cases in connection with northern Uganda, four in connection with the Democratic Republic of Congo (DRC), and one in connection with the Central African Republic (CAR). In contrast to Sudan, which has resisted ICC jurisdiction, these three countries are states parties to the ICC; all three and referred situations in their countries to the Prosecutor. Four suspects are currently in ICC custody, all Africans: Jean-Pierre Bemba, Thomas Lubanga, Germain Katanga, and Mathieu Ngudjolo. No one has yet been convicted by the ICC.

Uganda[84]

The government of Uganda, a party to the ICC, referred "the situation concerning the Lord's Resistance Army" to the Court in 2003.[85] The Lord's Resistance Army (LRA) is a rebel group that has fought for over two decades in northern Uganda. In October 2005, the ICC unsealed arrest warrants — the first issued by the Court — for LRA leader Joseph Kony and LRA commanders Vincent Otti, Okot Odhiambo, Dominic Ongwen, and Raska Lukwiya. The Prosecutor accused the LRA of establishing "a pattern of brutalization of civilians," including murder, forced abduction, sexual enslavement, and mutilation, amounting to crimes against humanity and war crimes.[86] None of the suspects are in custody; Lukwiya and Otti have reportedly been killed since the warrants were issued, while other LRA commanders are reportedly in hiding in eastern Democratic Republic of Congo. While Uganda's referral specifically mentioned the Lord's Resistance Army, the Prosecutor also is investigating alleged crimes committed by the Ugandan military in northern Uganda.

Despite widespread documentation of LRA abuses, the ICC's actions in Uganda have met with some strong domestic and international opposition due to debates over what would constitute justice for the war-torn communities of northern Uganda and whether the ICC has helped or hindered the pursuit of a peace agreement.[87] Some observers argue that ICC arrest warrants were a crucial factor in bringing the LRA to the negotiating table in 2006 for peace talks brokered by the Government of South Sudan. In August 2006, rebel and government representatives signed a landmark cessation of hostilities agreement; in February 2008, the government and the LRA reached several significant further agreements, including a permanent cease-fire. However, threats of ICC prosecution are considered by some to be a stumbling block to achieving an elusive final peace deal. The LRA has reportedly demanded that ICC arrest warrants be annulled as a prerequisite to a final agreement. The Ugandan government has offered a combination of amnesty and domestic prosecutions for lower- and mid-ranking LRA fighters, and is reportedly willing to prosecute LRA leaders in domestic courts if the rebels accept a peace agreement. This could entail challenging the LRA cases' admissibility before the ICC under the principle of complementarity. However, only the ICC's Pre-Trial Chamber has the authority to make a decision on admissibility. The ICC Prosecutor has reportedly stated that he will fight any move to drop the LRA prosecutions.[88]

Democratic Republic of Congo (DRC)

The DRC government referred "the situation of crimes within the jurisdiction of the Court allegedly committed anywhere in the territory of the DRC" to the Prosecutor in April 2004.[89] Despite the end of a five-year nationwide civil war in 2003 and the conduct of national elections in 2006, the DRC has continued to suffer from armed conflict, particularly in the volatile eastern regions bordering Rwanda, Uganda, and Burundi. The ICC has issued four arrest warrants in its first DRC investigation, which focuses on the eastern Congolese district of Ituri, where an inter-ethnic war erupted in June 2003 with reported involvement by neighboring governments.[90] Three suspects are in custody, while a fourth remains at large. The Prosecutor has stated that a second investigation in the DRC will focus on sexual crimes committed in the eastern provinces of North and South Kivu, while a third will look into "the role of those who organized and financed" armed groups throughout the country.[91] The latter investigation could potentially target officials from neighboring countries as well as members of the Congolese government and armed forces.[92]

Thomas Lubanga Dyilo

The ICC issued a sealed arrest warrant in February 2006 for Thomas Lubanga Dyilo, the alleged founder and leader of the *Union des Patriotes Congolais* (UPC) in Ituri and its military wing, the *Forces Patriotiques pour la Libération du Congo* (FPLC). At the time, Lubanga was in Congolese custody and had been charged in the domestic justice system.[93] After a determination of admissibility by the ICC, Lubanga was transferred to ICC custody in March 2006. The ICC has charged Lubanga with three counts of war crimes related to the recruitment and use of child soldiers.[94] Despite anticipation that the case would lead to a straightforward conviction, in June 2008, prior to trial, the ICC Trial Chamber stayed the proceedings against Lubanga because the Prosecutor had allegedly failed to disclose exculpatory evidence.[95] On July 2, Lubanga was ordered released. A preliminary application by the Prosecutor to lift the stay of proceedings was rejected by the ICC Trial Chamber in early September 2008. A final decision on whether to proceed with Lubanga's trial is pending, during which time the accused is to remain in custody.[96]

Germain Katanga and Mathieu Ngudjolo Chui

Germain Katanga, the alleged highest-ranking commander of the *Force de Résistance Patriotique en Ituri* (FRPI) and Ngudjolo, the alleged highest-ranking commander of the *Front des Nationalistes et Intégrationnistes* (FNI), are being prosecuted as co-perpetrators for allegedly having "acted in concert to mount an attack targeted mainly at Hema civilians" in Ituri in 2003.[97] The ICC issued sealed arrest warrants for Katanga and Ngudjolo in July 2007, and they were transferred by Congolese authorities to ICC custody in October 2007 and February 2008, respectively. The Prosecutor has accused them jointly of four counts of crimes against humanity and nine counts of war crimes related to murder, "inhumane acts," sexual crimes, the use of child soldiers, rape, and other abuses.[98] The case is in the pre-trial phase.

Bosco Ntaganda

The ICC issued a sealed warrant for the arrest of Bosco Ntaganda, the alleged former Deputy Chief of General Staff for Military Operations in Lubanga's FPLC, in August 2006. In April 2008, the ICC unsealed the warrant, having determined that public knowledge of ICC proceedings would neither endanger witnesses nor further obstruct attempts to bring Ntaganda into custody.[99] The ICC Prosecutor has accused Ntaganda of three counts of war crimes related to the alleged recruitment and use of child soldiers in 2002 and 2003.[100] Attempts to arrest Ntaganda have been complicated by the fact that he is reportedly currently serving as second-in-command in another rebel group, the *Con grès National pour la Défence du Peuple* (CNDP), in the DRC's North Kivu province. The CNDP, currently the DRC's most significant rebel organization, is led by Laurent Nkunda, a dissident military general.[101] Ntaganda remains at large.[102]

Central African Republic (CAR)

The government of CAR, a party to the ICC, referred "the situation of crimes within the jurisdiction of the Court committed anywhere on [CAR] territory"to the ICC Prosecutor in January 2005.[103] In May 2008, the ICC issued a sealed warrant of arrest for Jean-Pierre Bemba Gombo, a former DRC rebel leader. The warrant alleged that as commander of the *Movement de Libération du Congo* (MLC), one of two main DRC rebel groups during that country's civil war, Bemba had overseen systematic attacks on civilians in CAR territory between October 2002 and March 2003.[104] The Prosecutor accused Bemba of five counts of war crimes and three counts of crimes against humanity for alleged rape, torture, pillaging, and other abuses.[105] Bemba, who had been in exile in Europe since 2007, was arrested by Belgian authorities in May 2008 and turned over to the ICC in July 2008.

Bemba's prosecution by the ICC has been controversial in the DRC, where the MLC is now the largest opposition party.[106] After serving as one of four vice-presidents in the DRC transitional government from July 2003 to December 2006, Bemba came in second in the DRC's 2006 presidential election with 42% of the vote, behind the incumbent president, Joseph Kabila; Bemba's supporters accused the president of electoral fraud. Bemba won a Senate seat in January 2007, but he went into exile the following April after relations with Kabila continued to deteriorate. Some observers consider Bemba's prosecution by the ICC to be politically expeditious for President Kabila, whose main rival is now in international custody. The Office of the Prosecutor has strenuously denied that political considerations played a role in the decision to pursue Bemba.[107]

ISSUES RAISED BY THE ICC'S ACTIONS IN AFRICA

Many observers have praised the ICC's investigations in Africa as a crucial step against widespread impunity on the continent. Nevertheless, the ICC' s actions have provoked debates over the court's potential impact, its perceived prioritization of Africa over other regions, its selection of cases, and the effect of international prosecutions on peace processes. Most persistently, critics have accused the ICC of potentially jeopardizing the settlement of long-running civil wars in the pursuit of an often abstract "justice." Supporters of the Court reject these criticisms, and hope that ICC investigations will build accountability for the world's gravest atrocities and contribute to Africa's long-term peace and stability.

Potential Impact

Many hope that the ICC will usher in a new period of international accountability for the gravest human rights abuses by ensuring that perpetrators are brought to justice. The ICC's founders anticipated that by ending impunity, the ICC would deter future atrocities.[108] Indeed, some observers have argued that the ICC's success should be evaluated not just based on the punishment of past atrocities, but also in terms of "the effect its investigations have on reducing abysmal conduct in the present and future."[109] (The Office of the Prosecutor maintains that the choice of cases is not based on calculations of deterrent effect, though the Office acknowledges that strategic communications related to ICC prosecutions may play a role in deterrence.[110]

The goal of deterrence has been particularly salient in the ICC's investigations in Africa, which have focused to-date on regions where conflict is ongoing or only recently settled.[111] However, difficulties in enforcing ICC arrest warrants and the fact that the Court has yet to convict any suspects have led some to question whether the threat of ICC prosecution is credible. Some observers suggest that the Court's failure to apprehend suspects in Darfur in particular has bared tensions between the ICC's universal mandate and its reliance on the enforcement power of states.[112] Others maintain that deterrence is difficult to evaluate and that changes in perpetrators' behavior may be visible only over the long-run. Some argue that the Court's compilation of evidence, including transcribed interviews with witnesses, may serve future prosecutions or reconciliation processes even if they do not immediately lead to convictions.

Accusations of Bias

The ICC' s investigations in Sub-Saharan Africa have stirred concerns over African sovereignty and the long history of foreign intervention on the continent. For example, President Paul Kagame of Rwanda, which is not a state party to the Court, has portrayed the ICC as a new form of "imperialism" that seeks to "undermine people from poor and African countries, and other powerless countries in terms of economic development and politics."[113] Other commentators have alleged that the Prosecutor has limited investigations to Africa because of geopolitical pressures, either out of a desire to avoid confrontation with major powers or as a tool of Western foreign policy.[114] The attempt to prosecute Bashir has been particularly controversial, drawing rebuke from African governments and regional organizations. Supporters of the Court respond that investigations to-date have been determined by referrals, either by African states or the Security Council, and that the Prosecutor is analyzing situations in countries outside of Africa. In addition, observers have pointed out that national legal systems in Africa are particularly weak, which has allowed the ICC to assert its jurisdiction under the principle of complementarity.[115] The Office of the Prosecutor maintains that its choice of cases is based on the relative gravity of abuses, and that crimes committed in Sub-Saharan Africa are among the world's most serious.[116]

The Prosecutor's selection of cases also has proven controversial. ICC prosecutions in Sudan had, prior to the request for a warrant against President Bashir, drawn criticism for targeting mid-level officials rather than those with alleged higher-order responsibility for abuses in Darfur. Some have criticized ICC prosecutions in Uganda, the DRC, and CAR for focusing on alleged abuses committed by rebel fighters to the exclusion of those reportedly committed by government troops. In Uganda, some observers suggest that the ICC is seen locally as closely associated with the administration of President Museveni, as only LRA commanders have been targeted since the Prosecutor's investigation in northern Uganda began despite reported abuses by government troops.[117] The decision to pursue DRC opposition leader Jean-Pierre Bemba Gombo has provoked accusations that the Prosecutor was swayed by political bias or excessive pragmatism. As one pair of authors has written, "perceptions of the ICC on the ground have at times been damaged by insufficient efforts by the Court to make clear the basis on which individuals have been the subject of warrants and of particular charges, while those of apparently equal culpability have not."[118] ICC supporters have responded that the Prosecutor is mandated to focus on a limited number of particularly serious cases, and that investigations are ongoing and could lead to prosecutions against members of opposing sides in the future.

Justice vs. Peace?

One of the most persistent criticisms of the ICC's actions in Africa has been that by prosecuting active participants in ongoing or recently settled conflicts, the Court risks prolonging violence or endangering fragile peace processes. By removing the bargaining chip of amnesty from the negotiating table, critics allege, the ICC may remove incentives for peace settlements while encouraging perpetrators to remain in power in order to shield themselves from prosecution. Some observe that in such cases, "it is difficult to tell victims of these conflicts that the prosecution of a small number of people should take precedence over a peace deal that may end the appalling conditions they endure and the daily risks they face."[119]

Concerns that the aims of "justice" and "peace" may conflict have been particularly prominent in Uganda and Sudan. In Uganda, some observers argue that ICC arrest warrants against LRA commanders have acted as an impediment to achieving a final peace agreement. However, others counter that the threat of ICC prosecution, on top of other shifts in the conflict, was a decisive factor in bringing the LRA to the negotiating table in 2006. This observation has led some to see the ICC in Uganda as "an important ingredient in a political solution" for the conflict-plagued north.[120] In Sudan, some observers have argued that the attempt to prosecute President Bashir could endanger the Comprehensive Peace Agreement for southern Sudan and the peace process in Darfur, or provide an incentive to the ruling party to cling to power ahead of elections scheduled for 2009. For example, according to former U.S. envoy to Sudan Andrew Natsios, "the regime will now avoid any compromise or anything that would weaken their already weakened position, because if they are forced from office they face trials before the ICC... [An

ICC warrant for Bashir] may well shut off the last remaining hope for a peaceful settlement for the country."[121] U.N. Secretary-General Ban Ki-moon, who has maintained a neutral position on the ICC's actions in Sudan, has nonetheless argued that the international community must seek to balance "peace" and "justice" in dealing with the conflict in Darfur.[122] On the other hand, some argue the ICC request for a warrant against Bashir has opened up new opportunities to secure a just peace in Darfur. Indeed, several see progress in the Sudanese ruling party's decision to reach out to its domestic political rivals, for example by appointing south Sudan's Vice President Kiir to head a government commission to coordinate the government's response to the ICC.[123] Moreover, U.S. officials, Darfur advocacy groups, and others have stated that justice and accountability are paramount aims in Sudan.

Supporters of international prosecutions maintain that the pursuits of peace and justice are complementary, rather than opposed, as a credible threat of prosecution may serve as an important lever of pressure on actors in a conflict.[142] For example, Priscilla Hayner of the International Center for Transitional Justice writes, "it would be wrong to suggest that pragmatism always trumps principle in matters of life and death, and thus that one must ease up on justice in order to achieve peace. In some cases, the interest of peace has been well served by strong, forthright efforts to advance justice."[125] Many observers have pointed out that discerning the effect of ICC actions on complex processes is extremely difficult. As Nick Grono and Adam O'Brien of the International Crisis Group observe, "peace deals that sacrifice justice often fail to produce peace" in the long-run.[126]

Implications for Future U.S. Policy on the ICC

It is unclear whether U.S. views on the acceptability of the ICC have changed as a result of events since July 14, 2008. The United States abstained on Council Resolution 1828 (2008), extending the UNAMID mandate, pointing to the language in a preambular paragraph that referred to the July 14 application by the ICC prosecutor and the possibility of a Council request for deferral of further consideration of ICC consideration of that case as the reason for the abstention. The United States also had abstained on Council Resolution 1593 (2005), by which the Council sent the situation in Darfur to the ICC for investigation. While the Bush Administration would have preferred a different venue for consideration of the genocide conditions in Darfur, it did not halt referral to the ICC by vetoing the resolution.

Some observers have suggested that the U.S. position in the past would not have permitted abstention on the two Council resolutions. Thus, they maintain that the United States has moved to a policy that recognizes that under·certain circumstances, the ICC may have a role.[127] Others have pointed out, however, that any perceived moderation in U.S. views toward the Court has not affected its overall position not to become a party to the ICC Statute.

Current U.S. efforts, as reflected by U.S. abstentions in the Council appear to be driven by non-ICC foreign policy issues that are perceived as more important. The need to support the U.S. policy against genocide in Darfur was perceived as more important than overall U.S. opposition to the ICC. This broader policy drove the U.S. abstention on Council referral of the situation to the ICC in 2005. Moreover, the need to ensure that the UNAMID mandate, on the brink of expiring, was extended for another 12 months was perceived as more important and drove the U.S. abstention in July 2008.

John Bellinger, the Legal Advisor to the Secretary of State, in a speech in April on the United States and the ICC, noted,

> Now it may strike some as a bit ironic that a senior U.S. Government official would speak at a conference "celebrating" the tenth anniversary of the International Criminal Court, given that the U.S. Government's concerns about the Court are so well known. But I welcome this opportunity to appear to share the U.S. Government's views. Indeed,· I will tell you up front that one of my main themes is that even if we disagree over the means chosen by the Rome Statute — and I believe that this is a disagreement that is likely to continue under future U.S. Administrations unless U.S. concerns are addressed — nevertheless we do not disagree over the Statute's end goals, and we are prepared to work with those who support the Court in appropriate circumstances.[128]

APPENDIX A. LIST OF AFRICAN STATES SHOWING WHETHER THEY ARE PARTIES TO THE ICC AND HAVE RATIFIED THE "ARTICLE 98 AGREEMENT"

Country	Party to ICC	Ratified Article 98 Agreement
Algeria		X
Angola		X
Benin	X	X
Botswana	X	X
Burkina Faso	X	X

Country	Party to ICC	Ratified Article 98
Burundi	X	X
Cameroon		X
Cape Verde		X
Central African Republic	X	X
Chad	X	X
Comoros	X	·X
Congo, Republic of	X	X
Congo, Democratic Republic of	X	X
Côte divoire		X
Djibouti	X	X
Egypt		X
Equatorial Guinea		X
Eritrea		X
Ethiopia		
Gabon	X	X
Gambia, The	X	X
Ghana	X	X
Guinea	X	X
Guinea-Bissau		X
Kenya[a]	X	·
Lesotho	X	X
Liberia	X	X
Libya		
Madagascar	X	X
Malawi	X	X
Mali[a]	X	
Mauritania		X
Mauritius	X	X
Morocco		X
Mozambique		X
Namibia[a]	X	
Niger[a]	X	
Nigeria	X	X
Rwanda		X
São Tomé and Príncipe		X
Senegal	X	X
Seychelles		X
Sierra Leone	X	X

(Continued).

Country	Party to ICC	Ratified Article 98 Agreement
Somalia		
South Africa[a]	X	
Sudan		
Swaziland		X

Sources: International Criminal Court; U.S. Department of State, *Treaties in Force 2007*.

Note: [a] Economic Support Fund (ESF) assistance to these countries, which are parties to the ICC but have not signed Article 98 agreements, remains restricted under the Nethercutt Amendment. However, the restriction was waived by President Bush in 2006 and 2008 (see report).

REFERENCES

[1]   Concurrent Resolution Declaring Genocide in Darfur, Sudan (H.Con.Res. 467 [108th]), agreed to by the House of Representatives and the Senate on July 22, 2004; White House Press Release, "President's Statement on Violence in Darfur, Sudan," September 9, 2004.

[2]   The ICC began operating at its inauguration on March 11, 2003. The ICC plans to define and determine its jurisdiction over Crimes of Aggression in 2009. The Statute also established a second independent institution, the Trust Fund for Victims, to help victims of these crimes. The Trust Fund for Victims can only act in situations where the ICC has jurisdiction.

[3]   For the current status of signatures, ratifications, and reservations, see the ICC's website, [http://www.icc-cpi.int/asp/statesparties.html].

[4]   For background information on the International Criminal Court, see CRS Report RL3 1437, *International Criminal Court: Overview and Selected Issues*, by Jennifer Elsea.

[5]   Articles 13 and 14 (1) of the Rome Statute provide for both States Parties and U.N. Security Council referral of "situations" to the Court. During the negotiations, the question arose of whether individual "cases" or "situations" should be referred to the ICC Prosecutor. According to one author, writing on the jurisdiction of the ICC, "it was suggested that States Parties should not be able to make complaints about individual crimes or cases: it would be more appropriate, and less political, if 'situations' were instead referred to the Court." (Elizabeth Wilmshurst, "Jurisdiction of the Court," Chapter 3, in Roy

S.Lee, editor, *The International Criminal Court. The Making of the Rome Statute: Issues, Negotiations, Results* [Boston: Kluwer Law International, 1999], p. 131.) Another author, writing on the role of the Prosecutor, noted that the "powers of the Prosecutor could also be broadened in the context of a State's complaint to the Court, if the complaint referred to 'situations' rather than to individual 'cases.'" A proposal to this effect, introduced by the U.S. delegation in 1996, was "very soon supported by a large majority of States," many of whom had been "uneasy" with allowing a party to "select individual cases of violations and lodge complaints...with respect to such cases. This could...encourage politicization of the complaint procedure." The Prosecutor, after referral of the situation, could "initiate a case against the individual or individuals concerned." (Silvia A. Fernandez de Gurmendi, "The Role of the International Prosecutor," Chapter 6, in Lee, *The International Criminal Court*, p. 180.)

[6]   See press releases on each referral at the ICC's website, [http://www.icc-cpi.int].

[7]   Reportedly, the ICC has received 1,700 communications about alleged crimes in 139 countries, but 80 percent have been found to be outside the jurisdiction of the court. The Prosecutor has received self referrals only from African countries. See Stephanie Hanson, Global Policy Forum, "Africa and the International Criminal Court," *Council on Foreign Relations*, July 24, 2008.

[8]   The bar for proving complementarity has been set very high. In the ICC case against Congolese suspect Thomas Lubanga Dyilo, the Pre-Trial Chamber ruled that in order for a case to be inadmissible, national proceedings must encompass "both the person and the conduct which is the subject of the case before the Court" (ICC Pre-Trial Chamber I, The Prosecutor Vs. Thomas Lubanga Dyilo, *Decision on the Prosecutor's Application for a Warrant of Arrest, Article 38*, February 10, 2006). This language suggests that a domestic prosecution must essentially duplicate the ICC prosecution in order for admissibility to be challenged. Even in such a case, the ICC may retain jurisdiction if domestic proceedings are not conducted impartially or independently (Rome Statute, Article 17).

[9]   Article 27 of the Rome Statute.

[10] The United States signed the Rome Statute under the Clinton Administration, on December 31, 2000, but the Statute was never ratified by the Senate. In May 2002, the Bush Administration notified the United Nations that it did not intend to become a party to the ICC, and that there were therefore no legal obligations arising from the signature.

[11] The United States had supported a version of the Rome Statute that would have allowed the U.N. Security Council to refer cases involving non-states parties to the ICC, but would not have allowed other states or the Prosecutor to refer cases.

[12] Each state party to an Article 98 agreement promises that it will not surrender citizens of the other state party to international tribunals or the ICC, unless both parties agree in advance. An Article 98 agreement would prevent the surrender of certain persons to the ICC by parties to the agreement, but would not bind the ICC if it were to obtain custody of the accused through other means. See Appendix A for a list of states parties to the ICC and Article 98 agreements in Africa.

[13] These prohibitions do not apply to cooperation with an *ad hoc* international criminal tribunal established by the U.N. Security Council such as the International Criminal Tribunal for the Former Yugoslavia (ICTY) or the International Criminal Tribunal for Rwanda (ICTR). See 22 U.S .C. 7423(a)(1). In the case of Darfur, the *Darfur Accountability and Divestment Act of 2007* (H.R. 180), passed by the House on August 3, 2007, would offer U.S. support to the ICC's efforts to prosecute those responsible for acts of genocide in Darfur.

[14] The creation of the ICC is the culmination of a decades-long effort to establish an international court with the jurisdiction to try individuals for the commission of crimes against humanity. For a general background and discussion of the ICC, see CRS Report RL30020, *The International Criminal Court Treaty: Description, Policy Issues, and Congressional Concerns*, by Ellen Grigorian; CRS Report RL3 1437, *International Criminal Court: Overview and Selected Legal Issues*, by Jennifer K. Elsea; and CRS Report RL32605, *Genocide: Legal Precedents Surrounding the Definition of the Crime*, by Judith Derenzo and Michael John Garcia.

[15] On May 25, 1993, U.N. Security Council Resolution 827 (1993) established the International Criminal Tribunal for the former Yugoslavia (ICTY). It had its precursors in U.N. Security Council Resolution 752, which asked parties to respect humanitarian law; U.N. Security Council Resolution 771, which condemned ethnic cleansing and demanded access by international observers; and U.N. Security Council Resolution 780, which requested the U.N. Secretary-General to establish a Commission of Experts to investigate alleged violations of humanitarian law.

[16] U.N. Security Council Resolution 935 (2004) asked the Secretary-General to establish a Commission of Experts to examine the allegations of genocide

and grave violations of international humanitarian law in Rwanda. After its investigation, the Commission recommended that an international tribunal be established to address the crimes. On November 8, 2004, the Security Council, in Resolution 955, established the International Criminal Tribunal for Rwanda (ICTR).

[17] See, for example, "African International Courts and Tribunals" website, at [http://www.aict-cita.org].

[18] The Special Court for Sierra Leone (SCSL), a hybrid international-domestic court based in Sierra Leone's capital, Freetown, was set up jointly by the Government of Sierra Leone and the United Nations under Security Council Resolution 1315 (2000). It is mandated to try those who bear the greatest responsibility for serious violations of international humanitarian law and Sierra Leonean law committed in the territory of Sierra Leone after November 30, 1996. While most suspects have been tried in Freetown, former President Charles Taylor of Liberia is in custody in the Hague, where he is being tried by the SCSL for crimes against humanity and other violations of international humanitarian law.

[19] See U.S. Department of State, *United States Participation in the United Nations—2006*, p. 130.

[20] See CRS Report RL34003, *Africa Command: U.S. Strategic Interests and the Role of the U.S. Military in Africa*, by Lauren Ploch. The Defense Department has signaled its intention to locate an AFRICOM staff presence on the continent, either in the form of a headquarters or regional offices. Depending on the country, the United States may or may not have a Status of Forces Agreement (SOFA) that appropriately covers military personnel not detailed to the Embassy. The United States also has a semi-permanent troop presence known as Combined Joint Task Force-Horn of Africa (CJTF-HOA), in Djibouti. Personnel associated with CJTF-HOA conduct activities throughout the region. The command authority for CJTF-HOA, currently under Central Command (CENTCOM), will be transferred to AFRICOM in late 2008.

[21] Presidential Determination No. 2006-27 of September 29, 2006; CRS interview with State Department official, September 4, 2008.

[22] Presidential Determination No. 2007-5 of November 27, 2006, waives restrictions on FY2006 ESF assistance; Presidential Determination No. 2008-2 1 of June 20, 2008, does not specify a fiscal year.

[23] S/RES/1564 (2004), September 18, 2004.

[24] *Report of the International Commission of Inquiry on Darfur to the United Nations Secretary-General*, S/2005/60, January 25, 2005.

[25] See U.N. Press Release, "Security Council Refers Situation in Darfur, Sudan, to Prosecutor of International Criminal Court," SC/8351; and U.N. Press Release, "Secretary- General Welcomes Adoption of Security Council Resolution Referring Situation in Darfur, Sudan to International Criminal Court Prosecutor," March 31, 2005, SG/SM/9797- AFR/1 132.

[26] U.N. Security Council Resolution 1593 (2005), March 31, 2005.

[27] Frederic L. Kirgis, "U.N. Commission's Report on Violations of International Humanitarian Law in Darfur: Security Council Referral to the International Criminal Court," *American Society of International Law Insight Addendum*, April 5, 2005.

[28] U.N. Press Release, "Security Council Declares Intention to Consider Sanctions to Obtain Sudan's Full Compliance with Security, Disarmament Obligations on Darfur," SC/8 191, September 18, 2004.

[29] U.S. Mission to the United Nations (USUN) Press Release #055, "Explanation of Vote on the Sudan Accountability Resolution," Ambassador Ann W. Patterson, March 31, 2005.

[30] See Paragraph 6 of Security Council Resolution 1593; also see Kirgis, Op. Cit.

[31] USUN Press Release #055, Op. Cit.; USUN Press Release #229, "Statement on the Report of the International Criminal Court," Carolyn Willson, Minister Counselor for International Legal Affairs, November 23, 2005.

[32] The Sudanese government has denied having control over the Janj aweed, a term for ethnic Arab militias accused of perpetrating human rights abuses in Darfur. However, consensus exists among human rights researchers, journalists, and others who have visited Darfur that the Janj aweed have received arms and support from the government.

[33] ICC Press Release, "Warrants of Arrest for the Minister of State for Humanitarian Affairs of Sudan, and a Leader of the Militia/Janjaweed," May 2, 2007.

[34] International Federation of Human Rights, "The International Criminal Court and Darfur: Questions and Answers," available online at [http://www.iccnow.org/documents/FIDH_QA_Darfur_ENG.pdf].

[35] See e.g. Human Rights Watch, *Lack of Conviction: The Special Criminal Court on the Events in Darfur*, June 2006; U.N. News, "Sudan's Special Court On Darfur Crimes Not Satisfactory, UN Genocide Expert Says," December 16, 2005.

[36] CRS interview with human rights researcher, September 10, 2008.

[37] ICC Office of the Prosecutor, *Seventh Report of the Prosecutor of the ICC to the UN Security Council pursuant to UNSC 1593 (2005)*, June 5, 2008.

[38] In a briefing to the Security Council on June 5, 2008, the ICC Prosecutor had indicated that he would present a second case on Darfur to ICC judges in July. ICC Office of the Prosecutor, *Seventh Report of the Prosecutor*, Op. Cit.

[39] The counts are: (1) Genocide by killing of members of each target group; (2) Genocide by causing serious bodily or mental harm to members of each target group; (3) Genocide by deliberately inflicting on each target group conditions of life calculated to bring about the group's physical destruction; (4) Murder of civilians in Darfur, constituting a crime against humanity; (5) Extermination by inflicting conditions of life calculated to bring about the destruction of a part of the civilian population in Darfur, constituting a crime against humanity; (6) Forcible transfer of population in Darfur, constituting a crime against humanity; (7) Torture of civilians in Darfur, constituting a crime against humanity; (8) Rape of civilians in Darfur, constituting a crime against humanity; (9) Attacks against the civilian population in Darfur, constituting a war crime; and (10) Pillaging of towns and villages in Darfur, constituting a war crime (ICC Office of the Prosecutor, *Summary of Prosecutor's Application under Article 58*, July 14, 2008).

[40] ICC Office of the Prosecutor, *Summary of the Case: Prosecutor's Application for Warrant of Arrest under Article 58 Against Omar Hassan Ahmad Al Bashir.*

[41] Rome Statute, Article 27. International legal experts are, however, divided as to whether the Rome Statute waives "procedural" immunity for sitting heads of state — i.e., protection from arrest while traveling to a foreign country in official capacity — under customary international law. For further discussion, see Marko Milanovic, "ICC Prosecutor Charges the President of Sudan with Genocide, Crimes Against Humanity and War Crimes in Darfur," *American Society of International Law Insight*, July 28, 2008; Dapo Akande, "The Bashir Indictment: Are Serving Heads of State Immune from ICC Prosecution?," *Oxford Transitional Justice Research Working Paper Series*, July 30, 2008; and Pondai Bamu, "Head of State Immunity and the ICC: Can Bashir be Prosecuted?" *Oxford Transitional Justice Research Working Paper Series*, August 1, 2008.

[42] Maggie Farley and Edmund Sanders, "Darfur Genocide Laid at Sudan President's Door," *The Chicago Tribune*, July 15, 2008. In late August, Bashir traveled to and from Turkey, which is not a party to the ICC.

[43] See CRS Report RL32605, *Genocide: Legal Precedent Surrounding the Definition of the Crime*, by Judith Derenzo and Michael John Garcia, for a discussion of the legal elements of genocide under the Rome Statute and under the 1948 Convention on the Prevention and Punishment of the Crime of Genocide.

[44] Darfur's main rebel groups are associated with these ethnicities; the Prosecutor's case against Bashir alleges that military and militia attacks specifically targeted civilians even where rebel locations were spatially separate and well-known.

[45] ICC Office of the Prosecutor, "Summary of the Case." The application for a warrant references reprisals against other, smaller ethnic groups in connection with alleged war crimes and crimes against humanity. The estimate of 35,000 killed is much lower than the figure of 200,000-400,000 referenced by some non-governmental organizations and researchers, though many of these estimates include deaths indirectly caused by the conflict.

[46] See e.g. Human Rights Watch, "Darfur: ICC Moves Against Sudan's Leader; Charges Against al-Bashir a Major Step to Ending Impunity," July 14, 2008; Amnesty International, "President Of Sudan Could Face Arrest Over Darfur War Crimes," July 18, 2008.

[47] *Report of the International Commission of Inquiry on Darfur to the United Nations Secretary-General Pursuant to Security Council Resolution 1564 of 18 September 2004*, January 25, 2005.

[48] E.g., Eric Reeves, "Report of the International Commission of Inquiry on Darfur: A critical analysis (Part II)," *Sudanreeves.org*, February 6, 2005.

[49] Alex de Waal, "Darfur, the Court and Khartoum: The Politics of State Non-Cooperation," in Nicholas Waddell and Phil Clark, eds., *Courting Conflict? Justice, Peace and the ICC in Africa* (London: The Royal Africa Society, March 2008). Another critical response is presented by Rony Brauman, "The ICC's Bashir Indictment: Law Against Peace," *World Politics Review*, July 23, 2008. For further background, see Human Rights Watch, *Entrenching Impunity: Government Responsibility for International Crimes in Darfur*, December 2005.

[50] E.g., BBC Monitoring, "Sudanese Leader Calls International Court 'Tool of Imperialist Forces,'" [State-owned] Suna News Agency, August 20, 2008.

[51] See e.g. *Al-Sahafah* [Khartoum], "Sudanese Aide Accuses West of Striving to Replace Al-Bashir," via BBC Monitoring, August 21, 2008; *Sudan*

Tribune, "Sudan Warns UN Chief Over ICC," via BBC Monitoring, August 18, 2008; and de Waal, Op. Cit.

[52] The Sudanese government signed the Rome Statute on September 8, 2000, but did not ratify it. On August 26, 2008, Sudan notified the Secretary-General of the United Nations, as depositary of Rome Statute of the International Criminal Court, that Sudan "does not intend to become a party to the Rome Statute. Accordingly, Sudan has no legal obligation arising from its signature on 8 September 2000." (Reference: C.N.612.2008.TREATIES-6 [Depositary Notification], Rome Statute of the International Criminal Court, "Sudan: Notification.")

[53] CRS interview with ICC Office of the Prosecutor official, September 3, 2008. ICC prosecutorial staff have conducted extensive interviews with witnesses outside of Sudan, including in neighboring countries.

[54] *The Associated Press* (hereafter, *AP*), "Sudan Dismisses ICC Proceedings on Darfur, Reiterates Refusal to Hand Over Any Suspects," July 11, 2008.

[55] Suliman Baldo, "The Politics of an Arrest Warrant," *Making Sense of Darfur* [online forum published by the Social Science Research Council], July 23, 2008.

[56] See e.g., transcript of Bashir' s press conference in Istanbul, Turkey, on August 20, 2008, via the Open Source Center.

[57] Abdelmoniem Abu Edries Ali, "Sudan Appoints Darfur Prosecutor," *Agence France-Presse* (hereafter, *AFP*), August 6, 2008.

[58] See e.g., *AP*, "Sudan: ICC Case Could Provoke Violence," July 13, 2008; *AP*, "Sudan Rejects Genocide Charges Against President, Lawmaker Says Sudan Can't Ensure U.N. Safety," July 14, 2008; Katharine Houreld, "Official: Aid workers might not be safe in Sudan if ICC issues arrest warrant for president," *AP*, July 22, 2008; BBC News Online, "Sudanese Warning on Peacekeepers," July 25, 2008; Daniel Bases, "Sudan Warns 'Consequences' Over Warrant - UN," *Reuters*, August 19, 2008; *AP*, "Sudan's President Says Ready To Go To War," August 20, 2008; *Akhbar al Yawm* [pro-government Sudanese newspaper], "Political Parties Support President's Decision on 'Expelling' UNAMID," via BBC Monitoring, August 24, 2008.

[59] Peter Clottey, "Sudan Denies Threatening U.N. Staff Over ICC Arrest Warrants," Voice of America, August 19, 2008; see also Mohamed Osman, "Darfur Peacekeepers' Chief: Sudan Cooperating," *AP*, August 21, 2008.

[60] U.N. Security Council, *Report of the Secretary-General on the Deployment of the African Union-United Nations Hybrid Operation in Darfur*, S/2008/558, August 18, 2008. The report states that the United Nations is

investigating who was behind the attack, and documents several other "direct attacks" on UNAMID personnel in July 2008.

[61] Lydia Polgreen and Jeffrey Gettleman, "Sudan Rallies Behind Leader Reviled Abroad," *The New York Times*, July 28, 2008; Sarah El Deeb, "Indicted Sudanese President Seeks Help From Rivals," *AP*, August 6, 2008. Bashir has stated that elections will take place as scheduled (Jennie Matthew, "Beshir Vows Sudan Elections on Time," *AFP*, August 3, 2008).

[62] *Reuters*, "Instant View: ICC Prosecutor Seeks Warrant for Sudan's Bashir," July 14, 2008; *AFP*, "'Delighted' Darfur Rebels Offer to Help Bring Beshir In," July 14, 2008.

[63] See e.g. "Sudan: Saving Omer," *Africa Confidential*, August 1, 2008; and Naseem Badiey, "Ocampo v Bashir: The Perspective from Juba," *Oxford Transitional Justice Research Working Paper Series*, July 18, 2008.

[64] SPLM Press Release, "SPLM Position On ICC Indictment," July 21, 2008; see also Wasil Ali, "SPLM Official Calls on Sudan to 'Deal Legally' With ICC," *Sudan Tribune*, August 15, 2008.

[65] SPLM Press Release, "SPLM Position On ICC Indictment"; SPLM Press Release, "SPLM Reviews ICC Indictment as 2nd PB Meeting Opens," July 26, 2008; Najum Mushtaq, "ICC Indictment Sparks Hope, Fear," *Inter Press Service*, July 18, 2008.

[66] Opheera McDoom, "Analysis-Justice Clashes With Peace on Darfur Bashir Warrant," *Reuters*, July 14, 2008; Mushtaq, Op. Cit.

[67] Milton Olupot, "Delay Arrest of Bashir — Kiir," *New Vision* [Kampala], July 23, 2008.

[68] United Nations Mission in Sudan (UNMIS) press review, July 15, 2008; see also *Sudan Tribune*, "Interview: Sudan FM expresses frustration with the ruling NCP over Darfur crisis," September 8, 2008.

[69] The OIC is an inter-governmental organization of 57 states that aims to "project the interests of the Muslim world" (OIC website, at [http://www.oic-oci.org/oicnew/page_detail.asp?p_id=52]).

[70] African Union, *Letter Dated 14 July 2008 from the Permanent Observer of the African Union to the United Nations Addressed to the President of the Security Council*, S/2008/465.

[71] Security Council Report, "Update Report: Sudan," July 28, 2008. While some see these statements as evidence of regional support for Bashir, others point out that the option of a deferral could serve as leverage over Khartoum.

[72] Jennie Matthew, "AU Recruiting Top Lawyers Over Sudan War Crimes Probe," *AFP*, August 5, 2008.

[73] *Reuters*, "Darfour - La CPI Complique les Choses, Selon le Médiateur Onu-UA," July 31, 2008; *AFP*, "Soudan: Ping rencontre Béchir, critique la procédure de la CPI," August 4, 2008.

[74] *Reuters*, "Developing States Worried by Sudan Indictment," July 31, 2008.

[75] Rodney Muhumuza, "We Can't Condemn ICC Over Bashir — Museveni," *The Monitor* [Kampala], August 4, 2008.

[76] See e.g., *The Daily Champion* [Lagos, Nigeria], "Al-Bashir's Indictment [editorial]," August 6, 2008; Paul Ejime, "Before Al-Bashir Goes on Trial," *The Guardian* [Lagos], July 28, 2008; Al-Jazeera, "The Opposite Direction," presented by Faysal al-Qasim, August 12, 2008, via the Open Source Center; *AFP*, "Praise and Criticism for ICC From African Rights Organizations," July 16, 2008.

[77] The U.N. Security Council requested that the Secretary-General report every 90 days on progress made in implementation of UNAMID and the status of the political process.

[78] Security Council Report, "Update Report, Sudan," July 28, 2008, available at [http://www.securitycouncilreport.org].

[79] David Scheffer, "The Security Council's Struggle over Darfur and International Justice," *Jurist* — Forum (Jurist, University of Pittsburgh School of Law), online at [http://jurist.law.pitt/forumy/2008/08/security-councils-struggle-over-darfur.php].

[80] Scheffer, Op. Cit. A more academic commentary on Article 16 may be found in Luigi Condorelli and Santiago Villalpando, *Referral and Deferral by the Security Council,* Chapter 17.2, in *The International Criminal Court: A Commentary*, edited by Antonio Cassese, Paola Gaeta, and John R.W.D. Jones (New York: Oxford University Press, 2002), vol. I, pp. 644-654.

[81] See S/PV.5947 for verbatim record of the meeting and U.N. Press Release S/9412 for an unofficial summary of the statements made and the text of the adopted resolution. For links to both items, see under July 31 at [http://www.un.org/Depts/dhl/resguide/scact2008.htm]. A U.S. vote against the resolution would have defeated the resolution since that "no" vote would have been a veto.

[82] Explanation of vote by Ambassador Alejandro Wolff, U.S. Deputy Permanent Representative, USUN Press Release # 209 (08), July 31, 2008. The text of preambular paragraph 9 follows: "Taking note of the African Union (AU) communiqué of the 142nd [AU] Peace and Security Council (PSC) Meeting dated 21 July (S/2008/481, annex), having in mind concerns raised by members of the Council regarding potential developments subsequent to the application by the Prosecutor of the International

Criminal Court of 14 July 2008, and taking note of their intention to consider these matters further."

[83] Remarks by Ambassador Alejandro Wolff, U.S. Deputy Permanent Representative, at the Security Council Stakeout [with the press], USUN Press Release #210 (08), July 31, 2008.

[84] See CRS Report RL3 3701, *Uganda: Current Conditions and the Crisis in North Uganda*, by Ted Dagne and Hannah Reeves.

[85] ICC Office of the Prosecutor Press Release, "President of Uganda Refers Situation Concerning the Lord's Resistance Army (LRA) to the ICC," January 29, 2004. According to an Office of the Prosecutor official, referrals by the governments of Uganda and DRC followed moves by the Office of the Prosecutor to open investigations under its discretionary power (CRS interview, September 3, 2008); see also Payam Akhavan, "The Lord's Resistance Army Case: Uganda's Submission of the First State Referral to the International Criminal Court," *The American Journal of International Law*, 99, 2 (April 2005), pp. 405-406.

[86] ICC Press Release, "Warrant of Arrest Unsealed Against Five LRA Commanders," October 14, 2005. Kony is wanted for 12 counts of crimes against humanity, including murder, enslavement, sexual enslavement, rape, and "inhumane acts," and 21 counts of war crimes, including murder, cruel treatment of civilians, directing an attack against a civilian population, pillaging, inducing rape, and the forced enlistment of children; the other LRA commanders are accused of crimes against humanity and war crimes, ranging from four to 32 counts.

[87] See Tim Allen, *Trial Justice: The International Criminal Court and the Lord's Resistance Army* (London: Zed Books, 2006).

[88] CRS interview with ICC Office of the Prosecutor official, September 3, 2008. According to the official, the Ugandan government has expressed continued commitment to arresting the LRA leaders in discussions with the ICC.

[89] ICC Office of the Prosecutor Press Release, "Prosecutor Receives Referral of the Situation in the Democratic Republic of Congo," April 19, 2004.

[90] Ituri' s armed groups did not participate in the peace process between DRC's major rebel movements that brought the country's nationwide civil war to an end in 2003. While U.N. peacekeepers and DRC government troops have succeeded in staunching much of the violence in Ituri, many of the groups have not disarmed, and the area is still considered unstable. See International Crisis Group, *Congo: Four Priorities for Sustainable Peace in Ituri*, Africa Report No. 140, May 13, 2008.

[91] ICC Press Release, "DRC: ICC Warrant of Arrest Unsealed Against Bosco Ntaganda," April 29, 2008.

[92] CRS interview with Office of the Prosecutor official, September 3, 2008. Nationals of non-member states are subject to ICC jurisdiction for crimes committed on the territory of a member state.

[93] According to Human Rights Watch, Lubanga was arrested by Congolese authorities after the killing of nine U.N. peacekeepers in Ituri in February 2005. He and other Ituri militia members had been charged with genocide, war crimes, and crimes against humanity, but had not been brought to trial when the ICC warrant was issued. (Human Rights Watch, "D.R. Congo: ICC Arrest First Step to Justice," March 17, 2006.)

[94] ICC, The Prosecutor Vs. Thomas Lubanga Dyilo, *Document Containing the Charges, Article 61(3)(a) (Public Redacted Version)*, August 28, 2006.

[95] For more information on the decision to stay proceedings, see Human Rights Watch, "International Criminal Court's Trial of Thomas Lubanga 'Stayed': Questions and Answers," at [http://hrw.org/english/docs/2008/ 06/1 9/congo 19163 .htm].

[96] ICC Press Release, "Trial Chamber I Maintains Stay of Proceedings in the Thomas Lubanga Dyilo Case," September 4, 2008.

[97] ICC, *Combined Factsheet: Situation in the Democratic Republic of the Congo, Germain Katanga and Mathieu Ngudjolo Chui*, June 27, 2008. Their cases were joined in March 2008.

[98] ICC, *Combined Factsheet*, Op. Cit.

[99] ICC Press Release, "Warrant of Arrest Against Bosco Ntaganda Unsealed," April 29, 2008.

[100] ICC Pre-Trial Chamber, The Prosecutor Vs. Bosco Ntaganda, *Warrant of Arrest*, August 22, 2006. The warrant states that Ntaganda is "believed to be" a Rwandan national.

[101] A peace deal was signed by Nkunda and other armed groups in North Kivu in January 2008, though reports indicate that sporadic fighting continues. For background on the conflict, see International Crisis Group, *Congo: Bringing Peace to North Kivu*, Africa Report No. 133, October 31, 2007.

[102] Jacques Kahorha , "Nkunda Rebuffs ICC Over Indictee," *Institute for War and Peace Reporting*, June 16, 2008.

[103] ICC Office of the Prosecutor Press Release, "Prosecutor Receives Referral Concerning Central African Republic," January 7, 2005.

[104] Bemba's MLC, based in the DRC's north, was reportedly invited into CAR by then-President Ange-Félix Patassé to help quell a rebellion led by

François Bozizé. Bozizé took power in a coup in 2003 and is the current president of CAR.

[105] ICC Press Release, "Surrender of Jean-Pierre Bemba to the International Criminal Court," July 3, 2008. The counts as listed in this document appear to have changed slightly from those listed in the original arrest warrant.

[106] The MLC converted itself into a political party following the end of the DRC civil war in 2003.

[107] CRS interview with Office of the Prosecutor official, September 3, 2008.

[108] Preamble of the Rome Statute; see also International Criminal Court Assembly of States Parties, "Court Adopts Agreements to Launch Court's Operation," United Nations Press Release L/3013, September 9, 2002.

[109] Waddell and Clark, "Introduction," in *Courting Conflict?*

[110] CRS interview, September 3, 2008.

[111] The ICC's temporal jurisdiction, which limits prosecution to crimes committed after the entry into force of the Rome Statute, has contributed to this phenomenon.

[112] See e.g. Kenneth A. Rodman, "Darfur and the Limits of Legal Deterrence," *Human Rights Quarterly*, 30, 3, August 2008.

[113] *AFP*, "Rwanda's Kagame says ICC Targeting Poor, African Countries," July 31, 2008; Rwanda Radio via BBC Monitoring, "Rwandan President Dismisses ICC as Court Meant to 'Undermine' Africa," August 1, 2008.

[114] See e.g. Oraib Al Rantawi, "A Step Forward or Backward?" *Bitter Lemons*, 32, 6, August 14, 2008.

[115] See e.g. Stephanie Hanson, "Africa and the International Criminal Court," *Council on Foreign Relations*, July 24, 2008.

[116] CRS interview with Office of the Prosecutor official, September 3, 2008.

[117] Michael Otim and Marieke Wierda, "Justice at Juba: International Obligations and Local Demands in Northern Uganda," in *Courting Conflict?* See also Tim Allen, Op. Cit. The Prosecutor is investigating alleged abuses by the Ugandan military. Observers agree, however, that alleged abuses by government troops are not equal in gravity to those reportedly committed by the LRA.

[118] Waddell and Clark, Op. Cit.

[119] Nick Grono and Adam O'Brien, "Justice in Conflict? The ICC and Peace Processes," in *Courting Conflict?*

[120] Akhavan, "The Lord's Resistance Army Case," Op. Cit.

[121] Quoted in Opheera McDoom, "Analysis: Justice Clashes With Peace on Darfur Bashir Warrant," *Reuters*, July 14, 2008.

[122] U.N. Security Council, *Report of the Secretary-General on the deployment of the African Union-United Nations Hybrid Operation in Darfur*, S/2008/558, August 18, 2008. Ban Ki-moon stated on August 28, 2008, that the Prosecutor's request for a warrant had "altered the political landscape, although it is too early to assess the impact it will have on the peace process" (Louis Charbonneau, "Peace in Sudan as Important as Justice — UN's Ban," *Reuters*, August 28, 2008).

[123] In early August 2008, the government withdrew troops from the town of Abyei, a flashpoint in the north-south conflict, a move that some see as proof that the NCP has chosen conciliation over confrontation in response to the arrest warrant request. In late August, Bashir visited Juba, the capital of South Sudan, for the first time in nearly two years. See *Oxford Analytica*, "International/Sudan: ICC Pursues Calculated Risk," August 6, 2008.

[124] E.g., Caroline Flintoft [International Crisis Group], "Our Silence on Sudan Shames Us," *The Globe and Mail*, June 16, 2008; Sara Darehshori [Human Rights Watch], "Doing the Right Thing for Darfur: An ICC indictment of Sudan's president serves peace and justice," *The Los Angeles Times*, July 15, 2008.

[125] Priscilla Hayner, "Seeking Justice as War Crimes Rage On," *The Chicago Tribune*, July 16, 2008.

[126] Grono and O'Brien, Op. Cit.

[127] See, for example, *Council on Foreign Relations*, "Bellinger Says International Court Flawed But Deserving of Help in Some Cases," Interview, July 10, 2007; *AP*, "U.S. Ambivalent on Genocide Charge Against Sudan's President, " *International Herald Tribune*, July 15, 2008; Hanson, Op. Cit.; and *Council on Foreign Relations*, "The Dilemma of International Justice," Interview, July 28, 2008.

[128] John B. Bellinger, "The United States and the International Criminal Court: Where We've Been and Where We're Going," Remarks to the DePaul University College of Law, Chicago, Illinois, April 25, 2008, available at [http://www.state.gov/s/l/rls/104053.htm].

In: International Criminal Court
Editor: Harry P. Milton, pp. 41-77

ISBN: 978-1-60692-723-6
© 2009 Nova Science Publishers, Inc.

Chapter 2

U.S. POLICY REGARDING THE INTERNATIONAL CRIMINAL COURT*

Jennifer K. Elsea

Legislative Attorney
American Law Division

ABSTRACT

One month after the International Criminal Court (ICC) officially came into existence on July 1, 2002, the President signed the American Servicemembers' Protection Act (ASPA), which limits U.S. government support and assistance to the ICC; curtails certain military assistance to many countries that have ratified the Rome Statute establishing the ICC; regulates U.S. participation in United Nations (U.N.) peacekeeping missions commenced after July 1, 2003; and, most controversially among European allies, authorizes the President to use "all means necessary and appropriate to bring about the release" of certain U.S. and allied persons who may be detained or tried by the ICC. The provision withholding military assistance under the programs for Foreign Military Financing (FMF) and International Military Education and Training (IMET) from certain States Parties to the Rome Statute came into effect on July 1, 2003. The 1 09th Congress reauthorized the Nethercutt Amendment as part of the FY2006 Consolidated Appropriations Act (H.R. 3057/P.L. 109-102). Unless waived by the President, it bars Economic Support Funds (ESF) assistance to countries that have not agreed to protect U.S. citizens from being turned over to the ICC for prosecution. H.R. 5522, as passed by the House of Representatives, would

---

* Excerpted from CRS Report RL31495, dated August 29, 2006.

continue the ESF restriction for FY2007. The Senate passed a measure as part of the 2007 National Defense Authorization Act (H.R. 5122, S. 2766) that would modify ASPA to end the ban on IMET assistance.

The ICC is the first permanent world court with nearly universal jurisdiction to try individuals accused of war crimes, crimes against humanity, genocide, and possibly aggression. While most U.S. allies support the ICC, the Bush Administration firmly opposes it and has renounced any U.S. obligations under the treaty. After the Bush Administration threatened to veto a United Nations Security Council resolution to extend the peacekeeping mission in Bosnia on the ground that it did not contain sufficient guarantees that U.S. participants would be immune to prosecution by the ICC, the Security Council adopted a resolution that would defer for one year any prosecution of participants in missions established or authorized by the U.N. whose home countries have not ratified the Rome Statute. That resolution was renewed through July 1, 2004, but was not subsequently renewed. In addition, the United States is pursuing bilateral "Article 98"agreements to preclude extradition by other countries of U.S. citizens to the ICC. However, in what some view as a sign that the Administration is softening its stance with respect to the ICC, the United States did not exercise its veto power at the Security Council to prevent the referral of a case against Sudan's leaders for the alleged genocide in Darfur.

This report outlines the main objections the United States has raised with respect to the ICC and analyzes ASPA and other relevant legislation enacted or proposed to regulate U.S. cooperation with the ICC. The report concludes with a discussion of the implications for the United States, as a non-ratifying country, as the ICC begins to take shape, as well as the Administration's efforts to win immunity from the ICC's jurisdiction for Americans. A description of the ICC's background and a more detailed analysis of the ICC organization, jurisdiction, and procedural rules may be found in CRS Report RL3 1437, *International Criminal Court: Overview and Selected Legal Issues*, by Jennifer K. Elsea.

INTRODUCTION[1]

July 1, 2002, marked the birth of the International Criminal Court (ICC), meaning that crimes of the appropriate caliber committed after that date could fall under the jurisdiction of the ICC. The ICC is the first global permanent international court with jurisdiction to prosecute individuals for "the most serious crimes of concern to the international community."[2] Since its creation, the ICC has received three referrals by States Parties, which involved allegations of war crimes in the Republic of Uganda, the Democratic Republic of Congo, and the Central African Republic.[3] The United Nations Security Council has also referred a situation to the

Prosecutor — allegations of atrocities occurring in Darfur, Sudan.[4] The Chief Prosecutor subsequently decided to open investigations into three of the referred cases: Democratic Republic of the Congo,[5] Republic of Uganda,[6] and Darfur, Sudan.[7] Currently, five arrest warrants have been issued by the Court, all in connection to the situation in Northern Uganda.[8]

The United Nations, many human rights organizations, and most democratic nations have expressed support for the ICC.[9] The Bush Administration, however, opposes it and in May, 2002, formally renounced any U.S. obligations under the treaty,[10] to the dismay of the European Union.[11] On August 2, 2002, President Bush signed into law the American Servicemembers' Protection Act (ASPA) to restrict government cooperation with the ICC. The Administration had earlier stressed that the United States shares the goal of the ICC's supporters — promotion of the rule of law — and does not intend to take any action to undermine the ICC.[12]

While the United States initially supported the idea of creating an international criminal court[13] and was a major participant at the Rome Conference,[14] in the end, the United States voted against the Statute.[15] Nevertheless, President Clinton signed the treaty December 31, 2000, at the same time declaring that the treaty contained "significant flaws" and that he would not submit it to the Senate for its advice and consent "until our fundamental concerns are satisfied."[16] The Bush Administration has likewise declined to submit the Rome Statute to the Senate for ratification, and has notified the U.N. Secretary General, as depositary, of the U.S. intent not to ratify the treaty.[17] The primary objection given by the United States in opposition to the treaty is the ICC's possible assertion of jurisdiction over U.S. soldiers charged with "war crimes" resulting from legitimate uses of force, and perhaps over civilian policymakers, even if the United States does not ratify the Rome Statute. The United States sought to exempt U.S. soldiers and employees from the jurisdiction of the ICC based on the unique position the United States occupies with regard to international peacekeeping.[18]

On June 30, 2002, the United States threatened to veto a draft U.N. resolution to extend the peacekeeping mission in Bosnia because the members of the Security Council refused to add a guarantee of full immunity for U.S. personnel from the jurisdiction of the ICC, a move that provoked strong opposition from ICC supporters concerned with the viability of that institution, and that also raised some concerns about the future of United Nations peacekeeping.[19] Ultimately, however, the Security Council and the U.S. delegation were able to reach a compromise and adopted unanimously a resolution requesting the ICC defer, for an initial period of one year, any prosecution of persons participating in U.N. peacekeeping efforts who are nationals of states not parties to the ICC.[20] The compromise reached by the Security Council did not provide permanent immunity for U.S. soldiers and officials from prosecution by the ICC; rather, it invoked article 16 of the Rome Statute[21] to defer potential prosecutions for one year. Some States Parties to the Rome Statute and other supporters have argued that article 16 was meant only to apply to specific cases and was not intended to permit a blanket waiver for citizens of a specific country. The U.N. Security Council adopted another resolution extending the deferral to July 1, 2004.[22] However, during the summer of 2004, opposition to extending the deferral through 2005 eventually led the Administration to drop its pursuit. The United States continues to pursue bilateral agreements to preclude extradition by other countries of U.S. citizens to the ICC.

This report outlines the main objections the United States has raised with respect to the ICC and analyzes the American Servicemembers' Protection Act (ASPA)[23] enacted to regulate U.S. cooperation with the ICC. The report discusses the implications for the United States, as a non-ratifying country, as the ICC begins to take shape, as well as the Administration's efforts to win immunity from ICC jurisdiction for Americans. A description of the ICC's background and a more detailed analysis of the ICC's organization, jurisdiction, and procedural rules may be found in CRS Report RL3 1437, *International Criminal Court: Overview and Selected Legal Issues*.

U.S. OBJECTIONS TO THE ROME STATUTE

The primary objection given by the United States in opposition to the treaty is the ICC's possible assertion of jurisdiction over U.S. soldiers charged with "war crimes" resulting from legitimate uses of force, or its assertion of jurisdiction over other American officials charged for conduct related to foreign policy initiatives. The threat of prosecution by the ICC, it is argued, could impede the United States in carrying out military operations and foreign policy programs, impinging on the sovereignty of the United States. Detractors of the U.S. position depict the objection as a reluctance on the part of the United States to be held accountable for gross human rights violations or to the standard established for the rest of the world.

Below, in bold type, are summarized some of the main objections voiced by U.S. officials and other critics of the Rome Statute. Each objection is followed by the counterpositions likely to be voiced by representatives of U.S. foreign allies that support the ICC, as well as a very brief discussion of the issue. This section is intended to familiarize the reader with the basic issues that comprise the current debate, and not to provide an exhaustive analysis of the issues.[24] None of the statements in the section below should be interpreted to represent the view of CRS, since CRS does not take positions on policy issues.

Issue #1 Jurisdiction over Nationals of Non-Parties

Only nations that ratify treaties are bound to observe them. The ICC purports to subject to its jurisdiction citizens of non-party nations, thus binding nonparty nations.[25] ICC supporters may argue that the ICC has jurisdiction over persons, not nations. Non-party states are not obligated to *do* anything under the treaty. Therefore, the Rome Statute does not purport to bind non-parties, although non-party states may cooperate or defend their own interests that may be affected by a pending case. ICC opponents, however, may point out that if individuals are charged for conduct related to carrying out official policy, the difference between asserting jurisdiction over individuals and over the nation itself becomes less clear.[26]

After all, it is arguably the policy decision and not the individual conduct that is actually at issue. The threat of prosecution, however, could inhibit the conduct of U.S. officials in implementing U.S. foreign policy. In this way, it is argued, the ICC may be seen to infringe U.S. sovereignty.

Some ICC supporters have asserted that the crimes covered by the Rome Statute are already prohibited under international law either by treaty or under the concept of "universal jurisdiction" or both; therefore, all nations may assert jurisdiction to try persons for these crimes. The ICC, they argue, would merely be exercising the collective jurisdiction of its members, any of which could independently assert jurisdiction over the accused persons under a theory of "universal jurisdiction"; the Nuremberg trials serve as an example of such collective jurisdiction.[27] ICC opponents may note that the existence of "universal jurisdiction" has been disputed by some academics, who argue that actual state practice does not provide as much support for the concept as many ICC supporters may claim.[28] However, ICC supporters note, the Rome Statute does not rely entirely on universal jurisdiction; certain pre-conditions to jurisdiction must be met, including the consent of either the State on whose territory the crime occurred or the State of nationality of the accused.[29] The United States is already party to most of the treaties that form the basis for the definitions of crimes in the Rome Statute, meaning U.S. citizens are already subject to the prohibitions for which the ICC will have jurisdiction.

ICC supporters may further argue that if the ICC could not assert jurisdiction over non-party States, so-called "rogue regimes" could insulate themselves from the reach of the ICC simply by not ratifying the Rome Statute. The purpose for creating the ICC would be subverted. The United States had proposed to resolve this problem by creating a mandatory role for the U.N. Security Council in deciding when the ICC should assert jurisdiction, but the majority of other countries refused to adopt such a rule on the stated grounds that it would mirror the uneven prosecution of war crimes and crimes against humanity under the present system of *ad hoc* tribunals.

Issue #2 Politicized Prosecution

The ICC's flaws may allow it to be used by some countries to bring trumped-up charges against American citizens, who, due to the prominent role played by the United States in world affairs, may have greater exposure to such charges than citizens of other nations.[30] ICC supporters argue that the principle of "complementarity" will ensure that the ICC does not take jurisdiction over a case involving an American citizen, unless the United States is unwilling or unable genuinely to investigate the allegations itself, a scenario some argue is virtually unthinkable. Some also take exception to the notion that Americans are more likely to be targeted for prosecution although many other countries that participate in peacekeeping operations, for example, are willing to subject their soldiers and officials to the jurisdiction of the ICC. Many U.S. opponents of the ICC express concern that the ICC will be able to second-guess a valid determination by U.S. prosecutors to terminate an investigation or decline to prosecute a person. It is not uncommon for unfriendly countries to characterize U.S. foreign policy decisions as "criminal." The ICC could provide a forum for such charges. Some ICC supporters dispute the likelihood of such an occurrence, and express confidence that unfounded charges would be dismissed.

A recent determination by the ICC' s Chief Prosecutor seems to demonstrate a reluctance to launch an investigation against the United States based on allegations regarding its conduct in Iraq. On February 9, 2006, the Chief Prosecutor issued a letter explaining his reasons for declining to launch an investigation despite multiple submissions by private groups urging action against the United States.[31] In addition to acknowledging the limits of the Court's jurisdiction, which he noted precluded pursuing charges based on the legality of the decision to invade,[32] the Prosecutor noted that the allegations about U.S. nationals' behavior during the Iraq occupation were "of a different order than the number of victims found in other situations under investigation," and concluded that the allegations were of insufficient gravity to warrant an investigation.[33]

Issue #3 the Unaccountable Prosecutor

The Office of the Prosecutor, an organ of the ICC that is not controlled by any separate political authority, has unchecked discretion to initiate cases, which could lead to "politicized prosecutions."[34] ICC supporters may counter that the ICC statute does contain some restraints on the Prosecutor, including a provision that the Prosecutor must seek permission from a pre-trial chamber to carry out a self-initiated prosecution, and a provision for removal of the Prosecutor by vote of the Assembly of States Parties.[35] The independence of the prosecutor, it is argued, is vital in order to ensure just results, free from political control. U.S. negotiators at the Rome Conference had pressed for a role for the U.N. Security Council to check possible "overzealous" prosecutors and prevent politicized prosecutions. The majority of nations represented at the Rome Conference took the view that the U.N. Security Council, with its structure and permanent members, would pose an even greater danger of "politicizing" ICC prosecutions, thereby guaranteeing impunity for some crimes while prosecuting others based on the national interests of powerful nations.

Issue #4 Usurpation of the Role of the U.N. Security Council

The ICC Statute gives the ICC the authority to define and punish the crime of "aggression," which is solely the prerogative of the Security Council of the United Nations under the U.N. Charter.[36] ICC supporters may argue that all States Parties will have the opportunity to vote on a definition of aggression after the treaty has been in effect for seven years, which definition must comport with the U.N. Charter, thereby preserving the role of the U.N. Security Council.[37] The ICC, under this view, is merely providing a forum for trying persons accused of committing "aggression" under international law. Opponents of the ICC, however, may argue that the lack of agreement among nations as to the definition of aggression suggests that any definition adopted only by a majority of member states of the ICC may not be sufficiently grounded in international law to be binding as *jus cogens*.[38] The U.N.

General Assembly adopted a resolution in 1974[39] addressing the definition of aggression, but it has only been invoked once by the Security Council.[40] The definition contains an enumeration of offenses included as possible aggression,[41] but leaves the determination to the Security Council.

Issue #5 Lack of due Process Guarantees

The ICC will not offer accused Americans the due process rights guaranteed them under the U.S. Constitution, such as the right to a jury trial. Supporters of the Rome Statute contend it contains a comprehensive set of procedural safeguards that offers substantially similar protections to the U.S. constitution.[42] Some also note that the U.S. Constitution does not always afford American citizens the same procedural rights. For example, Americans may be tried overseas, where foreign governments are not bound to observe the Constitution. Moreover, cases arising in the armed services are tried by court-martial, which is exempt from the requirement for a jury trial. The current U.S. policy about the use of military tribunals in the war against terrorism could lead to suggestions of a double standard on the part of the United States with respect to procedural safeguards in war crimes trials.

CONGRESSIONAL ACTION

Congress has passed several riders effectively precluding the use of funds to support the ICC.[43] The 107th Congress passed the American Servicemembers' Protection Act of 2002 (ASPA) as title II of the supplemental appropriations bill for 2002, which was signed by the President on August 2, 2002.[44] The 108th Congress included a provision in the Consolidated Appropriations Act, P.L. 108-447, to prohibit the use of funds made available under the Economic Support Fund heading to provide assistance to countries who are members of the ICC and who have not entered into a so-called "Article 98" agreement with the United States. This provision, known as the Nethercutt Amendment, was reauthorized by the 109th Congress as part of the FY2006 Consolidated Appropriations Act (H.R. 3057/P.L. 109-102). A substantially identical provision is included in H.R. 5522, The Foreign Operations, Export Financing, and Related Programs Appropriations Act, 2007, as passed by the House of Representatives (§ 572).

American Servicemembers' Protection Act of 2002

Both the House of Representatives and the Senate added the American Servicemembers' Protection Act (ASPA) to the supplemental appropriations bill for the fiscal year ending September 30, 2002, H.R. 4775, 107th Congress. The conferees adopted the Senate version of the bill, which included a new provision that the ASPA will not prevent the United States from cooperating with the ICC if it prosecutes persons such as Saddam Hussein or Osama bin Laden.[45]

Legislative History
Originally introduced in the 106th Congress as S. 2726, the ASPA is intended to shield members of the United States Armed Forces and other covered persons from the jurisdiction of the ICC. The Senate Committee on Foreign Relations held hearings[46] the same day the bill was introduced but did not report it.

Prohibitions and Requirements
The ASPA prohibits cooperation with the ICC by any agency or entity of the federal government, or any state or local government. (Section 2004) Covered entities are prohibited from responding to a request for cooperation by the ICC or providing specific assistance, including arrest, extradition,[47] seizure of property, asset forfeiture, service of warrants, searches, taking of evidence, and similar matters.[48] It prohibits agents of the ICC from conducting any investigative activity on U.S. soil related to matters of the ICC. Section 2004(d) states that the United States "shall exercise its rights to limit the use of assistance provided under all treaties and executive agreements for mutual legal assistance in criminal matters ... to prevent ... use by the [ICC of such assistance]." It does not ban the communication to the ICC of U.S. policy, or U.S. government assistance to defendants. It does not prevent private citizens from providing testimony or evidence to the ICC. Section 2006 requires the President to put "appropriate procedures" in place to prevent the direct or indirect transfer of certain classified national security information to the ICC.[49]

Restrictions on Participation in Peacekeeping Missions
Unless subject to a blanket waiver under section 2003,[50] section 2005 of the ASPA restricts U.S. participation in U.N. peacekeeping operations to missions where the President certifies U.S. troops may participate without risk of prosecution by the ICC because the Security Council has permanently exempted U.S. personnel from prosecution for activity conducted as participants,[51] or because each other country in which U.S. personnel will participate in the mission is either not a party to the ICC and does not consent to its jurisdiction, or has entered into an agreement "in accordance with Article 98" of the Rome Statute.[52] The latter option may not provide as much assurance as the first; an Article 98 agreement would prevent the surrender of certain persons to the ICC by parties to the Article 98 agreement,[53] but would not bind the ICC if it were to obtain custody of the accused through other means. If the alleged crime is committed on the territory of a

state party to the Rome Statute, the consent requirement for the jurisdiction of the ICC would be met, despite the existence of the Article 98 agreement. That country could, however, carry out its own investigation and invoke complementarity to preclude the ICC's jurisdiction. Additionally, the country that is the object of the peacekeeping mission may consent to the ICC's jurisdiction over U.S. participants for alleged crimes committed on its territory, whether or not it is a member of the ICC.

The restriction may also be waived for peacekeeping missions where the President certifies that U.S. participation is in the national interest of the United States. The national interest qualification would appear to be the most easily met of the three waiver options; whenever the United States uses its vote in the Security Council to approve a peacekeeping operation, the mission presumably is deemed to serve the national interest.[54] This section could conceivably be interpreted to suggest the President has the authority to commit U.S. troops to participate in U.N. peacekeeping missions without the prior approval of Congress. The restriction does not apply to peacekeeping missions established prior to July 1, 2003.[55]

Restriction on Provision of Military Assistance

Effective 1 July 2003, the ASPA also prohibits military assistance to any country that is a member of the ICC, except for NATO countries and major non-NATO allies,[56] unless the President waives the restriction (section 2007) or a blanket waiver is in effect under section 2003. Military assistance, as defined in the ASPA, includes foreign assistance under chapters 2 and 5 of Part II of the Foreign Assistance Act of 1961, as amended,[57] and defense articles and services financed by the government, including loans and guarantees, under section 23 of the Arms Export Control Act.[58] The President may waive the prohibition without prior notice to Congress if he determines and reports to the appropriate committees that such assistance is important to the national interest or the recipient country has entered into a formal Article 98 agreement to prevent the ICC's proceeding against U.S. personnel present in such country.

The restriction does not appear to apply to any regional organizations that may receive military assistance. The restrictions on military assistance will no longer apply to these countries if they agree to sign Article 98 agreements with the United States, or if the President waives the restrictions as he deems justified with respect to a particular country in accordance with national interests.

One hundred countries are reported to have signed Article 98 agreements with the United States as of May 3, 2005.[59] It is not clear whether all of the agreements have been ratified by their respective governments so as to be effective at present.

Authority to Free Persons from ICC

Section 2008 authorizes the President to use "all means necessary and appropriate" to bring about the release of covered United States and allied persons,[60] upon the request of the detainee's government, who are being detained or imprisoned by or on behalf of the ICC. The Act does not provide a definition of "necessary and appropriate means" to bring about the release of covered persons, other than to exclude bribes and the provision of other such incentives. Section 2008 also authorizes the President to direct any federal agency to provide legal representation and other legal assistance, as well as any exculpatory evidence on behalf of covered U.S. or allied persons who are arrested, detained, investigated, prosecuted or imprisoned by, or on the behalf of the ICC. Section 2008 further permits the government to appear before the ICC in defense of the interests of the United States.

Waivers and Exceptions

The ASPA contains multiple waiver provisions and exceptions. Section 2003(a)-(b) provides for presidential waivers of sections 2005 and 2007 (restriction on U.S. participation in U.N. peacekeeping missions and prohibition on military assistance) if the President certifies to Congress that the ICC has agreed not to seek to assert jurisdiction over any covered U.S. or allied person with respect to actions undertaken by such person in an official capacity. This blanket waiver may be extended for successive periods of one year if the ICC abides by the agreement. As described above, section 2005 may be waived under its own terms with respect to specific peacekeeping missions if satisfactory protection can be achieved through U.N. Security Council measures or by agreement with other participants, or if the national interests of the United States justify participation in the mission.[61] Section 2007 also contains its own waiver provision, allowing the President to provide military assistance to a particular country if he determines and reports to Congress that it is in the national interest or that the country in question has entered into an agreement with the United States "pursuant to Article 98 of the Rome Statute preventing the International Criminal Court from proceeding against United States personnel present in such country."[62] NATO and major non-NATO allies are excepted from the prohibition in section 2007.[63]

If the ICC enters into and abides by an agreement under sections 2003(a) or (b), section 2003(c) permits the President to waive sections 2004 and 2006 (prohibiting cooperation with the ICC and directing the President to implement measures to prohibit the transfer of classified information) with respect to specific cases before the ICC. To waive the prohibitions and allow cooperation with the ICC, the President must first certify to Congress that there is reason to believe the accused is guilty as charged, it is in the national interest to waive the prohibitions, and that the investigation and prosecution by the ICC will not result in the investigation or arrest of any covered U.S. or allied persons with respect to any actions undertaken by them in an official capacity. It is somewhat unclear what a waiver of section 2006 would entail, in that the section does not directly prohibit any action. Instead, it directs the President to implement rules to prevent transfer of classified national security information and law enforcement information to the ICC, and to prevent indirect transfer of material related to matters under investigation or prosecution by the ICC to the United Nations and ICC member countries unless assurances are received from the recipient that such information will not be made available to the ICC. A waiver of section 2006 could be interpreted to mean that the President's requirement to implement the rules is waived, or that the requirement to obtain assurances from recipients other than the ICC is waived, or that the rules themselves may be waived with respect to a particular case.

Section 2011 provides an exception for certain presidential authorities, stating that the restrictions on cooperation with the ICC (section 2004) and the requirement for procedures to protect certain sensitive information (section 2006) do not apply to "any action or actions with respect to a specific matter taken or directed by the President on a case-by-case basis in the exercise of the President's authority as Commander in Chief of the Armed Forces of the United States under article II, section 2 of the United States Constitution or in the exercise of the executive power under article II, section 1 of the United States Constitution."[64] The section would require the President to notify Congress within 15 days of the action, unless such notification would jeopardize national security. It further clarifies that "nothing in [the] section shall be construed as a grant of statutory authority to the President to take any action."[65] Section 2012 prohibits delegation of the authorities vested in the President by sections 2003 (waiver provision) and 2011(a) (constitutional exception).[66]

Inasmuch as sections 2004 and 2006 are already subject to presidential waiver under section 2003(c) in the case of the investigation or prosecution of a "named individual," it appears that this section is drafted to avoid possible conflicts of the separation of powers between the President and Congress. In the event that the President takes the position that the prohibitions of sections 2004 and 2006 infringe upon his constitutional authority in certain cases, he might assert that Congress has no power even to require a waiver under section 2003. Section 2011 appears to ensure notification of Congress, at least at some point after the action has been taken, regardless of whether the President believes that sections 2004 and 2006 impinge his constitutional authority.

The effect of section 2011 is not entirely clear, depending as it does on the interpretation of the President's executive powers under article II, section 1 of the Constitution and his authority as Commander in Chief of the Armed Forces. Interpreted broadly, the constitutional executive power includes the power to execute the law, meaning the execution of *any* law, whether statutory or constitutional, or even international law. Such an interpretation would seem to render sections 2004 and 2006, as well as the waiver provision of section 2003(c), largely superfluous.[67]

Interpreted narrowly, the executive authorities cited above could refer to those powers which the President does not share with Congress. Under a narrow interpretation, Congress would be deemed to be without authority to regulate such actions in any event, in which case it would appear to make little sense to restrict its application to sections 2004 and 2006. The language could be construed by a court to imply a waiver authority apart from the restrictions outlined in section 2003.

Section 2015 provides clarification with respect to assistance to international efforts. It states:

> Nothing in this title shall prohibit the United States from rendering assistance to international efforts to bring to justice Saddam Hussein, Slobodan Milosovic, Osama bin Laden, other members of Al Qaeda, leaders of Islamic Jihad, and other foreign nationals accused of genocide, war crimes or crimes against humanity.[68]

This language would appear to have the effect of limiting the prohibitions in section 2004 to cases in which the ICC prosecutes non-U.S. citizens for the crimes currently under the jurisdiction of the ICC, although the United States may be obligated to deny such assistance in the case of an accused foreign national who is a national of a country with which the United States has entered into a reciprocal Article 98 agreement. The provision could also eliminate the restrictions on participation in peacekeeping missions or provision of military assistance where such participation or aid could be interpreted to further an international effort to prosecute the named crimes. There is no definition of "foreign national" in the ASPA; its use in section 2015 could lead to a conflict with sub-sections (d) and (f) of section 2004 (22 U.S.C. § 7423) as they apply to permanent resident aliens.

Reporting Requirements

In addition to the congressional notifications required by some of the waiver authorities described above, the ASPA encourages the President to submit, by February 2, 2003, a report for each military alliance to which the United States is a party assessing the command arrangements they entail and the degree to which such arrangements may place U.S. servicemembers under the command or control of foreign officers subject to the jurisdiction of the ICC.[69] No later than August 2, 2003, the President was encouraged to submit a report describing possible modifications to such alliance command arrangements that would reduce the risks to U.S. servicemembers identified in the first report.[70]

The Nethercutt Amendment

Section 574 of the FY2005 Consolidated Appropriations Act (H.R. 481 8/P.L. 108-447) prohibited Economic Support Funds (ESF) assistance to the government of any country that is a party to the ICC that has not entered into an Article 98 agreement with the United States, except for countries eligible for assistance under the Millennium Challenge Act of 2003. It authorized the President to waive the prohibition with respect to NATO members and major non-NATO allies without prior notice to Congress, if he determined and reported to the appropriate committees that a waiver was in the U.S. national security interest. The President could also waive the prohibition on economic assistance for countries that entered into Article 98 agreements with the United States. (Presumably, this provision would have applied to countries that later agreed to enter into such an Article 98 agreement, to ensure congressional notification).

The Nethercutt Amendment was re-enacted by the 109th Congress as part of the FY2006 Consolidated Appropriations Act (H.R. 3057/P.L. 109-102). The FY2006 measure, however, requires that the President give Congress notice before he invokes a waiver, but he may grant a waiver not only with respect to any NATO or major non-NATO ally, but also to "such other country as he may determine if he determines and reports to the appropriate congressional committees that it is important to the national interests of the United States to waive such prohibition." The Foreign Operations Appropriations bill for FY2007 (H.R. 5522), recently passed by the House of Representatives, would continue these prohibitions (§ 572). As with prior years' legislation, the bill would not affect the funding for the Millennium Challenge Corporation. The Senate Appropriations Committee reported its version of the bill without any similar prohibition.[71]

National Defense Authorization Act for FY2007

The Senate passed a measure as part of the 2007 National Defense Authorization Act, S. 2766, that would modify ASPA to end the ban on International Military Education and Training (IMET) assistance to countries that are members of the ICC and that have not implemented Article 98 agreements (§ 1210). The House version of the FY2007 Defense Authorization bill, H.R. 5122, does not contain such a provision; however, after hearing testimony from several combatant commands regarding the perceived negative consequences flowing from the cut-off of IMET assistance to affected allies, the House Armed Services Committee reported its view that the President's authority to waive ASPA funding restrictions can and should be invoked where necessary to "impede undue influence on U.S. partner nations" by third-party governments that might occur in the absence of U.S. engagement efforts made possible through IMET.[72]

Prospective Legislation

Some observers have suggested that Congress should pass legislation to close jurisdictional gaps in U.S. criminal law in order to ensure U.S. territory does not become a safe haven for those accused of genocide, war crimes, and crimes against humanity.[73] The War Crimes Act of 1 996,[74] for example, establishes U.S. federal jurisdiction to punish war crimes, as defined in international treaties to which the United States is a party, but only when perpetrated by or against U.S. nationals. Likewise, the Genocide Convention Implementation Act of 1987 prohibits acts that would constitute genocide under the Rome Statute, except that the U.S. Code covers only conduct committed by a U.S. national or conduct committed within the United States.[75] Some observers have expressed concern that war criminals or perpetrators of genocide from other countries could seek refuge in the United States from extradition to and prosecution by the ICC. However, the exception in section 2013 of the ASPA, which allows U.S. entities to cooperate with the ICC in the case of foreign nationals accused of war crimes, may obviate the need for such legislation.

Some have suggested that changes in U.S. statutes to broaden the jurisdiction of federal courts to cover all crimes over which the ICC might assert jurisdiction could enhance the implementation of complementarity by precluding a finding by the ICC that the United States is "unable" to prosecute one of its citizens.[76] For the most part, war crimes committed by U.S. persons are covered by the War Crimes Act, although there may be some acts covered by the Rome Treaty that are not explicitly prohibited by U.S. law. Also, there is no U.S. statute codifying crimes against humanity as such. U.S. criminal law prohibits most of the crimes enumerated under the Rome Statute as possible crimes against humanity, as long as they are committed within the United States or by military personnel.[77] Under current law, acts that could constitute crimes against humanity committed by U.S. civilians overseas generally are not triable in U.S. civil or military courts unless they involve torture or certain acts of international terrorism.[78] In the event a U.S. citizen is alleged to have committed such an act, the United States may not be deemed able to investigate and prosecute the alleged crime, a prerequisite for asserting complementarity.

IMPLICATIONS OF THE ICC FOR THE UNITED STATES AS A NON-MEMBER

As a member of the Preparatory Commission established by the Rome Statute, the United States played a significant role during the drafting of rules of procedure, elements of crimes, and other documents detailing how the ICC will operate. Now that the Rome Statute has entered into force, the Preparatory Commission has been replaced by the Assembly of States Parties ("Assembly") as the governing body to oversee the implementation of the Rome Statute. The Assembly held its first conference September 3 - 10, 2002, during which it adopted rules of evidence and procedure and a host of other regulations, including the methods for nominating and electing its officials. During its subsequent session in February, the Assembly elected 18 judges, who later elected Canadian jurist Philippe Kirsch to be their president. In April of 2003, the Assembly elected Argentinian lawyer Luis Moreno Ocampo to be the ICC's first prosecutor.

The first Review Conference, an alternative forum for considering amendments to the Statute, is to be convened in July of 2009, seven years after the Statute has entered into effect.[79] Thereafter, Review Conferences may be convened from time to time by the U.N. Secretary-General upon request by a majority of the States Parties.[80] As a non-party, the United States has no vote in either body. However, it will remain eligible to participate in both the Assembly and in Review Conferences as an observer.[81]

Observer Role

The Assembly of States Parties adopted procedural rules for its activities at its first conference, including rules setting forth the role of observers and other participants.[82] Observers are entitled to participate in the deliberations of the Assembly and any subsidiary bodies that might be established. Observer States will receive notifications of all meetings and records of Assembly proceedings on the same basis as States Parties. They will not, however, be permitted to suggest items for the agenda or to make motions during debate, such as points of order or motions for adjournment. Thus, the United States may be able to participate substantially in Assembly debates as well as proffer and respond to proposals, even if it never becomes a party to the Statute.[83] The United States may also use its position at the United Nations to communicate to the Assembly of States Parties.[84]

As noted, the United States is not able to vote in these bodies so long as it does not ratify the Rome Statute. It may not nominate U.S. nationals to serve as judges or cast a vote in elections for judges or the Prosecutor (or for their removal), or vote on the ICC' s budget. It will not be able to vote on the definition of the crime of aggression or its inclusion within the jurisdiction of the ICC, when the matter is considered at first Review Conference, or on any other amendment to the Rome Statute, unless it ratifies the Rome Statute.

The United States, as a non-party, will have no right itself to refer situations to the Prosecutor for investigation; as a Permanent Member of the Security Council, however, it could seek to influence referrals by the Security Council.[85] Similarly, it may participate in Security Council requests to the Prosecutor to defer an investigation or prosecution[86] and to the Pre-Trial Chamber to review a decision of the Prosecutor not to investigate or prosecute.[87] As a non-party to the treaty, the United States is eligible, but not obligated, to cooperate with any ICC investigation and prosecution;[88] and under the Statute, the United States could, but would not be obligated to, arrest a person named in a request for provisional arrest or for arrest and surrender from the ICC.[89] The United States also retains the right not to provide information or documents the disclosure of which would prejudice its national security interests[90] and to refuse to consent to the disclosure by a state party of information or documents provided to that state in confidence.[91] Finally, as a nonparty, the United States is not under any obligation to contribute to the budget for the ICC, except, perhaps indirectly, to the extent that the U.N. General Assembly regular budget might include ICC support.[92]

Foreign Policy Implications

Perspectives differ on the impact of the ICC on U.S. interests, as it begins to operate. Some see the ICC as a fundamental threat to the U.S. armed forces, civilian policy makers, and U.S. defense and foreign policy.[93] Others see it as a valuable foreign policy tool for defining and deterring crimes against humanity, a step forward in the decades-long U.S. effort to end impunity for egregious mass crimes. Debate over the ICC has created a tension between enhancing the international legal justice system and encroaching on what some countries perceive as their legitimate use of force. The review by the International Criminal Tribunal for the Former Yugoslavia (ICTY) of allegations that NATO bombing in Kosovo might be deemed a war crime is illustrative of this tension. Many opponents of the ICC were outraged that the issue was even considered. They questioned the legitimacy of the tribunal's actions, and their anger was not assuaged by the Tribunal's ultimate decision that there was "no basis for opening an investigation into any of those allegations or into other incidents relating to NATO bombing."[94] While opponents of the ICC interpret this event as an indication that the ICC is likely to pursue spurious and politically motivated cases against U.S. citizens, proponents of the ICC see it as illustrating that similar allegations would be dismissed by the ICC Prosecutor.

Another consideration is the practical effect that the U.S. position will have on the ICC itself. Because the ICC relies largely on States Parties to provide mechanisms and manpower for arresting suspects and enforcing verdicts of the ICC, it has been argued that the lack of U.S. participation in the ICC may seriously impair the ICC's ability to function.[95] Those who believe the ICC is a fundamental threat to U.S. foreign and defense policy may welcome this outcome; while ICC supporters may argue that an ineffective court could serve the interests of human rights abusers, ensuring impunity and decreasing the likelihood of future *ad hoc* tribunals.

The United States has enjoyed a long reputation for leadership in the struggle against impunity and the quest for universal human rights and the rule of law. Human rights organizations have expressed concern that U.S. refusal to ratify the Rome Statute, coupled with any actions that might undermine the ICC, could cause the United States to lose the moral high ground and damage its influence world-wide, including its ability to influence the development of the law of war.[96] The perceived U.S. willingness to hold U.N. peacekeeping missions hostage to U.S. demands for immunity from the ICC may deepen the rift between the United States and allies that support the ICC. The withholding of military assistance and other economic aid to members of the ICC may also be seen as an effort to coerce countries to refuse to ratify the Rome Statute or to sign an Article 98 agreement, which could appear to some as undermining the ICC and negating the Administration's stated intent to respect the decisions of other countries to join the ICC. By seemingly demanding special treatment in the form of immunity from the ICC, the United States may bolster the perception of its unilateral approach to world affairs and its unwillingness to abide by the same laws that apply to other nations. This perception could undermine U.S. efforts at coalition-building to gain international support for the present war against terrorism and operations in Iraq, as well as future international endeavors.[97]

Others argue that the perception of U.S. commitment to the rule of law has little effect on countries where human rights abuses are most rampant. Despots like Cambodia's Pol Pot or Iraq's Saddam Hussein have not weighed possible future legal ramifications before committing massive crimes.[98] Under this view, the establishment of the ICC might have the unintended effect of hardening the resolve of ruthless tyrants who may feel they have nothing to gain by giving up their power to more democratic regimes if they fear prosecution for the crimes they committed while in power. From this perspective, in terms of curbing human rights abuses, it does not matter whether the U.S. ratifies the Rome Statute, other than perhaps to provide support to an accused dictator's argument challenging the legitimacy of the ICC. According to this viewpoint, the costs to the United States appear to outweigh the benefits.

Strategy for Precluding ICC
Prosecution of U.S. Troops and Officials

ASPA § 2005 prohibits U.S. participation in peacekeeping and peace-enforcing missions established by the Security Council unless the President certifies and reports to the appropriate committees of Congress that U.S. personnel are not placed at risk of prosecution by the ICC because they are guaranteed immunity by the U.N. Resolution or because of arrangements with the host government.[99] The Bush Administration has pursued efforts in the U.N. Security Council and with individual States to prevent the possibility that American citizens could be prosecuted before the ICC. This effort has met with some success but also some resistance.

Agreement with the U.N. Security Council

On July 12, 2002, in response to the U.S. veto of the extension of peacekeeping operations in Bosnia, the U.N. Security Council adopted a resolution requesting a blanket deferral of prosecutions by the ICC of peacekeepers from states not parties to the Rome Statute for a period of one year. Resolution 1422 provides, in pertinent part:

Acting under Chapter VII of the Charter of the United Nations,

1   *Requests*, consistent with the provisions of Article 16 of the Rome Statute, that the ICC, if a case arises involving current or former officials or personnel from a contributing State not a Party to the Rome Statute over acts or omissions relating to a United Nations established or authorized operation, shall for a twelve-month period starting 1 July 2002 not commence or proceed with investigation or prosecution of any such case, unless the Security Council decides otherwise;

2   *Expresses* the intention to renew the request in paragraph 1 under the same conditions each 1 July for further 12-month periods for as long as may be necessary;

3   *Decides* that Member States shall take no action inconsistent with paragraph 1 and with their international obligations;

4   *Decides* to remain seized of the matter.[100]

The resolution, which was renewed for another year under Security Council Resolution 1487, appeared to fall short of the President's original proposal, which would have provided permanent immunity for U.S. troops and officials from the jurisdiction of the ICC. Opponents of the original proposal objected that the U.N.

Security Council does not have the authority to "rewrite" international treaties. The compromise invoked article 16 of the Rome Statute, which provides:

No investigation or prosecution may be commenced or proceeded with under this Statute for a period of 12 months after the Security Council, in a resolution adopted under Chapter VII of the Charter of the United Nations, has requested the Court to that effect; that request may be renewed by the Council under the same conditions.

Although some opponents of the U.S. position had argued that article 16 was intended to be invoked only on a case-by-case basis, the language of the article does not expressly state such a requirement. Therefore, Resolutions 1422 and 1487 appear to be consistent with the Rome Statute. The language deferred ICC action for one year; it does not provide absolute immunity for actions occurring during the deferral period. Because the Security Council did not extend the deferral past July 2004, it appears that the ICC may investigate and prosecute any purported crimes under its subject matter jurisdiction that occurred at any time after the Rome Statute's entry into force, subject to other provisions of the Rome Statute.

Other U.N. Missions

U.S. military personnel were able to participate in the United Nations Mission in Liberia (UNMIL) because, in authorizing the multinational force to enforce the cease-fire, the Security Council decided that

> current or former officials or personnel from a contributing State, which is not a party to the Rome Statute of the International Criminal Court, shall be subject to the exclusive jurisdiction of that contributing State for all alleged acts or omissions arising out of or related to the Multinational Force or United Nations stabilization force in Liberia, unless such exclusive jurisdiction has been expressly waived by that contributing State.[101]

Unlike the previous arrangement with respect to the U.N. mission in Bosnia, the authorization for operations in Liberia appears to provide permanent immunity to U.S. participants from the jurisdiction of the ICC with respect to conduct linked to the U.N. mission. Accordingly, President Bush made the appropriate certification to Congress under ASPA § 2005 (22 U.S.C. § 7424).[102] Liberia had signed the Rome Statute in 1998 but did not ratify it until September of 2004.

The United States also sent troops to participate in the U.N. mission to establish peace in Haiti in 2004.[103] In April of 2004, the U.N. Security Council established the United Nations Stabilization Mission in Haiti (MINUSTAH).[104] In June of that year, President Bush certified that U.S. servicemembers could safely participate because Haiti had signed an Article 98 agreement.[105]

U.N. Action Regarding the Situation in Darfur

On March 31, 2005, the U.N. Security Council, acting under Chapter VII of the U.N. Charter, adopted Resolution 1593 (2005) which refers reports about the situation in Darfur, Sudan (dating back to July 1, 2002), to the ICC Prosecutor, Luis Moreno-Ocampo.[106] This is the first time such a referral from the U.N. Security Council has been made. As Sudan is not a party to the ICC, and has not consented to its jurisdiction, the ICC jurisdiction over the case could only be established by means of a U.N.S.C. referral. Under the ICC Statute, the ICC is authorized, but not required, to take such a case. [107] The Resolution, which is binding on all U.N. member states, was adopted by a vote of 11 in favor, none against and with 4 abstentions — the United States, China, Algeria, and Brazil.[108]

U.S. foreign policy respecting action to address the situation in Darfur was complicated by its position regarding the ICC and its jurisdiction over non-member states. In September 2004, the United States concluded that genocide had taken place in Darfur. According to the State Department, it supported the formation of the International Commission of Inquiry[109] but preferred a tribunal in Africa to be the mechanism of accountability for those who committed crimes in Darfur. After these proposals failed to garner sufficient support, the United States agreed to abstain from voting on the Resolution (which is not equivalent to a veto in the U.N. Security Council) once language was introduced into the Resolution that dealt with the sovereignty questions of concern and essentially protected U.S. nationals and other persons of non-party States outside Sudan from prosecution.[110]

The abstention did not change the fundamental objections of the United States to the ICC. Although some view the decision as a sign that the Administration is softening its stance with respect to the ICC,[111] it may also be seen as consistent with the U.S. support of a version of the Rome Statute that would have allowed the U.N. Security Council to refer cases involving non-States Parties to the ICC, but would not have allowed other states to refer cases. At the same time, the compromise allowed the United States to show support for the need for the international community to come together and take action on the atrocities occurring in Darfur.[112]

Article 98 Agreements

The United States is also pursuing bilateral options for achieving protection for U.S. troops, within or outside U.N. peacekeeping arrangements, by concluding agreements similar to the status-of-forces agreements (SOFA) routinely negotiated where U.S. troops are stationed abroad. The United States has so far concluded 100 bilateral agreements whereby each signatory promises that it will not surrender citizens of the other signatory to the ICC, unless both parties consent in advance to the surrender.[113] The Department of State is seeking to conclude these agreements with as many states as possible, even those who are not parties to the ICC and others who would not be subject to the sanctions under ASPA.

The agreements are intended to make use of Article 98 of the Rome Statute, which states:

Cooperation with respect to waiver of immunity and consent to surrender

1   The Court may not proceed with a request for surrender or assistance which would require the requested State to act inconsistently with its obligations under international law with respect to the State or diplomatic immunity of a person or property of a third State, unless the Court can first obtain the cooperation of that third State for the waiver of the immunity.

2   The Court may not proceed with a request for surrender which would require the requested State to act inconsistently with its obligations under

international agreements pursuant to which the consent of a sending State is required to surrender a person of that State to the Court, unless the Court can first obtain the cooperation of the sending State for the giving of consent for the surrender.[114]

Paragraph 1 of Article 98 appears intended to retain diplomatic immunity and immunity for heads of state, while paragraph 2 seems to contemplate typical SOFA arrangements, in which countries hosting members or units of the armed forces of allies agree to forego certain types of jurisdiction over the soldiers and other government officers stationed there. The use of the term "sending state" in the second paragraph appears to indicate that it is meant to cover only persons who are sent to accomplish government business, and not citizens present in the country for personal or business reasons. The State Department reportedly sought broader application for the bilateral agreements. In 2002, the European Council argued that parties to the ICC who signed such agreements with the United States would be acting inconsistently with their obligations under the Rome Statute.[115] The European Union (EU), all of whose members are parties to the Rome Statute, initially opposed the agreements altogether, but its members reached a compromise to allow member countries to sign.[116] The EU issued guidelines for member countries for the acceptable terms of Article 98 agreements, specifying that coverage would be limited to government representatives on official business, the United States would expressly pledge to prosecute any war crimes committed by Americans, and the agreements would not contain a reciprocal promise to prevent the surrender of European citizens to the ICC.[117] In response to the Nethercutt Amendment, the European Council released a statement calling on President Bush to make "full use of his waiver authority" and reiterated the EU stand with respect to Article 98 agreements, referring to the 2002 guidelines.[118]

Despite the EU compromise, the U.S. pursuit of "immunity" has been criticized by some as unnecessary or as an outright effort to undermine the ICC.[119] Supporters of the policy note that agreements, such as SOFAs, that provide immunity for soldiers from prosecution in foreign courts are not unusual. For example, the 19- member International Security Assistance Force (ISAF), a joint force authorized by the U.N. Security Council to provide assistance to the interim government in Afghanistan,[120] included a clause providing immunity for participants in its Military Technical Agreement with the interim government.[121] Furthermore, supporters point out, the agreements are based on and consistent with Article 98 of the Rome Statute, and therefore cannot be said to undermine the ICC.

The practical effect of the Article 98 agreements is as of yet uncertain. The use of such agreements with host countries does not provide absolute immunity from the ICC. They would bind only countries that choose to sign, and would have the effect only of preventing the host nation from surrendering an accused to the ICC for prosecution. While the Rome Statute gives some discretion to States Parties to honor their international obligations applicable to extradition of persons who are identified in an ICC request for surrender,[122] there does not appear to be a provision for accused persons or their states of nationality to challenge the jurisdiction of the ICC based on the violation of a bilateral agreement. Therefore, States Parties to the Rome Statute are not precluded from entering into Article 98 agreements that provide for immunity of foreign troops from surrender, but if the ICC were nevertheless to gain custody over the accused through other means, its jurisdiction may not be affected by the agreement.

Options

Though the Administration continues to seek to conclude Article 98 agreements with relevant countries, it is not clear how many more such agreements are likely to be forthcoming. To strengthen the Administration's pursuit of these agreements, Congress could make more forms of aid contingent on the recipient country's agreement to protect U.S. troops from surrender to the ICC, or it could enact legislation to restrict the President's discretion to grant waivers. If further negotiations fail to garner necessary support, or in case the agreements should turn out to less effective than desired or counterproductive for other reasons, policymakers may seek alternative avenues. One option might be to implement a policy of investigating, and if warranted, prosecuting, all crimes under the ICC jurisdiction alleged to be committed by a U.S. person, thus preempting the ICC through application of the complementarity principle. Such a policy, coupled with changes in U.S. statutes to broaden the jurisdiction of federal courts to cover all relevant crimes, could further insulate U.S. citizens from the reach of the ICC. The United States could seek to further enhance its reputation for conducting fair and credible investigations and trials of suspected war criminals, as well as perpetrators of crimes against humanity or genocide, through the use of consistent procedures that are as open as security considerations permit. Such a practice may help to overcome any charges that a U.S. investigation or prosecution of an accused is not "genuine" for the purposes of complementarity.

Finally, some have argued that a policy of cooperation with the ICC in the prosecution of persons accused of crimes that the United States agrees amount to "the most serious crimes of concern to the international community"[123] would enhance the reputation of the United States as a promoter of human rights and the rule of law. Such a policy could take the form of passive non-interference with the ICC to active assistance, including working from within the U.N. Security Council to refer cases to the ICC. By actively keeping the Security Council involved in the referral of cases, some of the predicted problems with referrals by States Parties or by the prosecutor could be minimized. On the other hand, some argue a cooperative posture with respect to the ICC in the case of foreigners while pursuing immunity for U.S. citizens would be perceived as a double standard.

REFERENCES

[1]   Emily Cowley, Law Clerk, contributed research assistance to this report.

[2]   *See* Rome Statute of the International Criminal Court, Preamble, U.N. Doc. A/CONF. 183/9 (1998)("Rome Statute"). These include genocide, crimes against humanity, war crimes, and potentially the crime of aggression, if the Assembly of States Parties is able to reach an agreement defining it. *Id.* art. 5(1). *See generally* International Criminal Court, *How Does the Court Work?* [http://www.icc-cpi.int/ataglance/whatistheicc/howdoesthe court work.html], (hereinafter *How the ICC Works*) (last visited June 8, 2006), explaining the two ways investigations are initiated in the ICC: (1) a situation may be referred to the Prosecutor by States Parties or the United Nations Security Council or (2) the Prosecutor may independently initiate investigations on the basis of information received from reliable sources, if, after examining the information, he determines that there is a reasonable basis to proceed with an investigation.

[3]   *See* International Criminal Court, Situations and Cases, [http://www.icc-cpi.int/cases.html] (last visited June 9, 2006); *see also* American University War Crimes Research Office, International Criminal Court Status Update, [http://www.wcl.american.edu/warcrimes/ icc.status.cfm] (June 9, 2006) (providing a time line of significant events at the ICC).

[4]   SC Res. 1593, U.N. Doc S/RES/1593 (2005); *see infra* note 106 and accompanying text; *How the ICC Works*, *supra* note 2.

[5]   Press Release, International Criminal Court, The Office of the Prosecutor of the International Criminal Court Opens its First Investigation (June 23, 2004) *available at* [http://www.icc-cpi.int/pressrelease_details&id=26&l=en.html](last visited June 14, 2006).

[6]   *See* Press Release, International Criminal Court, The Prosecutor of the International Criminal Court Opens an Investigation into Northern

Uganda (July 29, 2004) *available at* [http://www.icc-cpi.int/pressrelease_details&id=33&l=en.html](last visited June 14, 2006).

[7] *See* Press Release, International Criminal Court, The Prosecutor of the ICC Opens Investigation in Darfur (June 6, 2006) *available at* [http://www.icccpi.int/pressrelease_details&id= 107& 1=en.html] (last visited June 14, 2006).

[8] *See* Situation in Uganda, Case No. ICC-02/04-01-05, Warrant of Arrest for Joseph Kony Issued on July 2005 as Amended on 27 September 2005, ¶ 42 (Sept. 27, 2005) *available at* [http://www.icc-cpi.int/library/cases/ICC-02-04-0 1-05-53_English.pdf] (last visited June 14, 2006) (charging Joseph Kony, the founder and leader of the Lord's Resistance Army (LRA), with 33 counts of war crimes and crimes against humanity); *see also Court Seeks Arrests of Ugandan Rebels*, N.Y. TIMES, Oct. 15, 2005, at A10 (reporting that warrants were issued for the arrest of four other senior leaders in addition to Joseph Kony).

[9] *See* Barbara Crossette, *World Criminal Court is Ratified — Praised by U.N., Opposed by U.S.*, N.Y. TIMES Apr. 12, 2002, *available at* 2002 WL-NYT 0210200003. As of Nov. 15, 2005, 100 nations have ratified the Rome Statute. For the current status of signatures, ratifications and reservations, visit [http://www .icc-cpi.int/asp/statesparties.html] (last visited June 14, 2006).

[10] *See* Jonathon Wright, *U.S. Renounces Obligations to International Court*, REUTERS, May 6, 2002. Although some in the media described the act as an "unsigning" of the treaty, it may be more accurately described as a notification of intent not to ratify. The U.S. letter to the U.N. Secretary General stated: This is to inform you, in connection with the Rome Statute of the International Criminal Court adopted on July 17, 1998, that the United States does not intend to become a party to the treaty. Accordingly, the United States has no legal obligations arising from its signature on December 31, 2000. The United States requests that its intention not to become a party, as expressed in this letter, be reflected in the depositary's status lists relating to this treaty. *See* U.N. Treaty Database, Rome Statute of the International Criminal Court, *available at* [http://untreaty.un.org/].

[11] The EU issued a statement at the Preparatory Commission for the International Criminal Court expressing "disappointment and regret," noting the "potentially negative effect that this particular action by the United States may have on the development and reinforcement of recent trends towards Individual accountability for the most serious crimes of concern to the international community and to which the United States shows itself

strongly committed." *See* Statement of the European Union on the position of the United States of America towards the International Criminal Court, U.N. Doc. PCNICC/2002/INF/7, May 20, 2002.

[12] *See* Marc Grossman, Under Secretary for Political Affairs, Remarks to the Center for Strategic and International Studies, Washington, D.C., (May 6, 2002), prepared remarks available at [http://www.state.gov/ p/9949.htm](last visited June 13, 2006). Secretary Grossman promised that: Notwithstanding our disagreements with the Rome Treaty, the United States respects the decision of those nations who have chosen to join the ICC; but they in turn must respect our decision not to join the ICC or place our citizens under the jurisdiction of the court. So, despite this difference, we must work together to promote real justice after July 1, when the Rome Statute enters into force. The existence of a functioning ICC will not cause the United States to retreat from its leadership role in the promotion of international justice and the rule of law.

[13] *See* Ruth Wedgwood, Harold K. Jacobson and Monroe Leigh, *The United States and the Statute of Rome,* 95 AM. J. INT'L L. 124 (2001) (commenting that the United States has "repeatedly and publicly declared its support in principle" for an international criminal court). Congress expressed its support for such a court, providing the rights of U.S. citizens were recognized. *See, e.g.,* Foreign Operations Appropriations Act § 599E, P.L. 101-513, 104 Stat. 2066-2067 (1990)(expres sing the sense of the Congress that "the United States should explore the need for the establishment of an International Criminal Court" and that "the establishment of such a court or courts for the more effective prosecution of international criminals should not derogate from established standards of due process, the rights of the accused to a fair trial and the sovereignty of individual nations"); Anti-Drug Abuse Act of 1988, § 4108, P.L. 100-690, 102 Stat. 4181, 4266 (1988)(encouraging the President to initiate discussions with foreign governments about the possibility of creating an international court to try persons accused of having engaged in international drug trafficking or having committed international crimes, providing constitutional guarantees of U.S. citizens are recognized); P.L. 99-399, § 1201 (1986) .

[14] See U.N. International Criminal Court: Hearings before the Subcomm. on International Operations of the Senate Foreign Relations Committee, 105th Cong. (1998) (testimony of David J. Scheffer, Ambassador-at-Large for War Crimes Issues).

[15] *See* Wedgwood *et al., supra* note 13, at 124 (noting that the final vote for the Statute was 120 in favor to seven against).

[16] *See* Statement on the Rome Treaty on the International Criminal Court, 37 WEEKLY COMP. PRES DOC 4 (Dec. 31, 2000).

[17] Because the United States signed the Rome Statute, it had been obligated under international law to refrain from conducting activity in contravention of the object and purpose of the treaty. *See* Vienna Convention on the Law of Treaties, *opened for signature* May 23, 1969, art. 18, 1155 U.N.T.S. 335. However, this obligation ends once a signatory state has indicated an intent *not* to ratify the treaty. *Id.*

[18] *See* Grossman, *supra* note 12. •

[19] See Colum Lynch, Dispute Threatens U.N. Role in Bosnia; U.S. Wields Veto in Clash over War Crimes Court, WASH. POST, Jul. 1, 2002, at A1.

[20] SC Res. 1422, U.N. Doc. S/RES/1422 (2002).

[21] *See infra* note 100, and accompanying text.

[22] SC Res. 1487, U.N. Doc. S/RES/1487 (2003). The vote was 12-0, with France, Germany and Syria abstaining.

[23] P.L. 107-206, title II, 116 Stat. 889 (2002), *codified at* 22 U.S.C. §§ 7421 *et seq.*

[24] For a more in-depth analysis of these issues, see CRS Report RL3 1437, *International Criminal Court: Overview and Selected Legal Issues*, by Jennifer K. Elsea.

[25] *See* Fact Sheet: The International Criminal Court, U.S. Department of State Office of War Crimes Issues, May 6, 2002; Grossman, *supra* note 12 (asserting "the United States has never recognized the right of an international' organization to [detain and try American citizens] absent consent or a U.N. Security Council mandate").

[26] See Ruth Wedgwood, The United States and the International Criminal Court: The *Irresolution of Rome*, 64 LAW & CONTEMP. PROBS. 193, 199 (2001) (arguing the state whose national is charged remains a "party in interest"to the prosecution).

[27] *See* Jordan J. Paust, *The Reach of ICC Jurisdiction over Non-Signatory Nationals*, 33 VAND. J. TRANSNAT'L L. 1, 3-4 (2000).

[28] *See* Wedgwood, *supra* note 26, at 199 (pointing out there is "no ordinary precedent for delegating national criminal jurisdiction to another tribunal, international or national, without consent of the affected states, except in the aftermath of international belligerency"). Some observers, however, note that one of the reasons for constituting an international criminal court was to do away with the need for military conquest prior to

prosecuting war crimes, in the hope of eliminating the perception of "victor's justice."

[29] Rome Statute, *supra* note 2, art. 12. *See generally* CRS Report RL3 1437, *International Criminal Court: Overview and Selected Legal Issues*, by Jennifer Elsea, at 21-26, (summarizing jurisdictional requirements). There is no consent requirement in cases referred by the Security Council.

[30] *See* Grossman, *supra* note 12.

[31] Letter from Luis Moreno-Ocampo, Chief Prosecutor, International Criminal Court, (Feb. 9, 2006) *available at* [http://www.icc-cpi.int/library/ organs/otp/OTP_letter_to_senders_ re_Iraq_9_February_2006.pdf]

[32] *See id.* at 3-4 (explaining that the ICC does not have personal jurisdiction over non-State Party nationals who performed the alleged crimes in a non-State Party territory).

[33] *See id.* at 9. The Prosecutor also seemed satisfied with U.S. efforts to investigate and prosecute possible war crimes: In light of the conclusion reached on gravity, it was unnecessary to reach a conclusion on complementarity. It may be observed, however, that the Office also collected information on national proceedings, including commentaries from various sources, and that national proceedings had been initiated with respect to each of the relevant incidents. *Id.*

[34] *See* Grossman, *supra* note 12.

[35] Rome Statute, *supra* note 2, art. 46, provides procedures for removing a Prosecutor who: Is found to have committed serious misconduct or a serious breach of his or her duties under [the Rome] Statute, as provided for in the Rules of Procedure and Evidence; or Is unable to exercise the functions required by this Statute.

[36] *See* Grossman, *supra* note 12.

[37] See CRS Report RL3 1437, *International Criminal Court: Overview and Selected Legal Issues*, by Jennifer Elsea, at 20-2 1 (summarizing issues relevant to the definition of "aggression").

[38] A mutually acceptable definition for the elements of the crime of aggression has long eluded the international community, impeding earlier attempts to establish an international criminal court. *See* Jimmy Gurulé, *United States Opposition to the 1998 Rome Statute Establishing an International Criminal Court: Is the Court's Jurisdiction Truly Complementary to National Criminal Jurisdictions?*, 35 CORNELL INT'L L.J. 1, 2 (2002). Article 39 of the U.N. Charter leaves

it to the Security Council to determine the existence of and take action with respect to any act of aggression, but does not provide a definition.

[39] G.A. Res. 3314, U.N. GAOR, 29th Sess., Supp. No. 19, U.N. Doc A/9615 (1974).

[40] *See* Kriangsak Kittichaisaree, *The NATO Military Action and the Potential Impact of the International Criminal Court*, 4 SING. J. INT'L & COMP. L. 498, 505 (2000) (citing U.N. Security Council Resolution 418 of 4 Nov. 1977, declaring South Africa guilty of aggression against Angola).

[41] G.A. Res. 3314, art. 3, lists the following examples of possible acts of aggression: The invasion or attack by the armed forces of a State of the territory of another State, or any military occupation, however temporary, resulting from such invasion or attack, or any annexation by the use of force of the territory of another State or part thereof; Bombardment by the armed forces of a State against the territory of another State or the use of any weapons by a State against the territory of another State; The blockade of the ports or coasts of a State by the armed forces of another State; An attack by the armed forces of a State on the land, sea or air forces, or marine and air fleets of another State; The use of armed forces of one State which are within the territory of another State with the agreement of the receiving State, in contravention of the conditions provided for in the agreement or any extension of their presence in such territory beyond the termination of the agreement; The action of a State in allowing its territory, which it has placed at the disposal of another State, to be used by that other State for perpetrating an act of aggression against a third State; The sending by or on behalf of a State of armed bands, groups, irregulars or mercenaries, which carry out acts of armed force against another State of such gravity as to amount to the acts listed above, or its substantial involvement therein.

[42] *See id.* at 29-38 (describing procedural safeguards in the Rome Statute); *see also* Selected Procedural Safeguards in Federal, Military, and International Courts, CRS Report RL3 1262 (providing brief comparison of ICC procedural safeguards to federal and military rules of procedure and evidence).

[43] *See* Department of Defense Appropriations for 2002, P.L. 107-117. § 8173. None of the funds made available in division A of this Act may be used to provide support or other assistance to the International Criminal Court or to any criminal investigation or other prosecutorial activity of the International Criminal Court. *See also* Departments of Commerce, Justice, and State, the Judiciary, and Related Agencies Appropriations

Act, 2002, § 630, P.L.107-77; 22 U.S.C. § 7401 (prohibiting appropriated funds from obligation for use by the ICC or to assist the ICC unless the United States becomes a party to the Rome Statute).

[44] P.L. 107-206, title II, 16 Stat. 899 (2002), *codified at* 22 U.S.C. §§ 7421 *et seq.*

[45] *See* H.R. REP. NO. 107-593 (2002).

[46] The International Criminal Court: Protecting American Servicemen and Officials from the Threat of International Prosecution, Hearing before the Senate Comm. on Foreign Relations, 106th Cong. (2000).

[47] The expenditure of funds for the extradition or transfer of U.S. citizens to countries that are obligated to surrender persons to the ICC is prohibited by 22 U.S.C. § 7402 unless the receiving country provides assurances that such citizen will not be surrendered to the ICC. The same prohibition applies with respect to giving consent to other countries to transfer or extradite U.S. citizens to States Parties of the ICC.

[48] 22 U.S.C. § 7423.

[49] 22 U.S.C. § 7425.

[50] 22 U.S.C. § 7422; *see infra* page 14.

[51] The compromise reached by the U.N. Security Council in Resolution 1422 (2002) provided for a one-year deferral, thus providing neither immunity nor permanent protection, which would not appear to meet this criterion. *See infra* note 100.

[52] 22 U.S.C. § 7424. The Rome Statute, *supra* note 2, art. 98, prohibits the ICC from pursuing requests for assistance or surrender that would require the requested state to act inconsistently with certain international obligations. This provision, as well as other provisions that refer to articles of the Rome Statute, may be seen as somewhat inconsistent with finding (11) of section 2, which states that the United States "will not be bound by any of [the terms of the Rome Statute]."

[53] Article 98 appears to cover only persons sent by the government to the requested state on official business, such as officials and military personnel, and would not cover private citizens who are present in the requested state for reasons unrelated to official duty. An agreement signed by a state party to the ICC that promises not to surrender any other citizens of another state to the ICC would appear to be covered by art. 97 of the Rome Statute, which requires the requested state to consult with the ICC if honoring a request for surrender to the ICC would cause the requested state to breach its international obligations. *See infra* note 113.

[54] *See, e.g.,* 22 U.S.C. § 287b(e)(2)(B) (requiring as part of an annual report to Congress on U.N. activities information about possible authorization for peacekeeping missions, including the "vital national interest to be served").

[55] 22 U.S.C. § 7424(b).

[56] Major non-NATO allies include Australia, Egypt, Israel, Japan, Jordan, Argentina, the Republic of Korea, and New Zealand. (§ 2007(d)). Taiwan is also exempt under § 2007. The President may designate other nations as major non-NATO allies under 22 U.S.C. § 232 1k, by notifying Congress 30 days in advance.

[57] 22 U.S.C. § 2151 *et seq.* Chapter 2 is codified at 22 U.S.C. §§ 2311 - 2321k (provision of defense articles and services). Chapter 5 is codified at 22 U.S.C. §§ 2347 - 2347d (international military education and training of foreign personnel in furtherance of the goals of international peace and security, to improve the recipient's self-defense capabilities, and to increase awareness of human rights).

[58] 22 U.S.C. § 2763 (authorizing President to provide credit to friendly foreign countries and international organizations for the purchase of defense articles and services).

[59] See Press Release, U.S. Department of State, U.S. Signs 100th Article 98 Agreement, May 3, 2005, *available at* [http://www.state.gov/r/pa/ prs/ps/2005/45573.htm](last visited June 14, 2006). For an unofficial list of signators, see Coalition for the ICC, Status of Bilateral Immunity Agreements (April 14, 2006), *available at* [http://www.iccnow.org/documents/ CICCFS_BIAstatusCurrent.pdf] (last visited June 14, 2006). For information regarding the application of the policy with respect to Latin American countries, see CRS Report RL33337, *Article 98 Agreements and Sanctions on U.S. Foreign Aid to Latin America*, by Clare M. Ribando.

[60] 22 U.S.C. § 7427. "Covered allied persons" include military personnel, elected or appointed officials, and other persons working for a NATO country or a major non-NATO ally, "so long as that government is not a party to the International Criminal Court and wishes its officials and other persons working on its behalf to be exempted from the jurisdiction of the [ICC]." 22 U.S.C. § 7432(3). Covered allies currently could include persons from the Czech Republic, Turkey, Egypt, Israel, Japan, the Republic of Korea, and Taiwan. All of these exempted countries are members of the ICC except the Czech Republic, Israel, Egypt, Turkey, Taiwan, and Japan. The Czech Republic, Egypt, and Israel signed the Rome Statute but have not

ratified it. In August of 2002, Israel notified the U.N. Secretary General that it does not intend to ratify the Rome Statute. ·

[61] 22 U.S.C. § 7424.

[62] 22 U.S.C. § 7426(c). "United States personnel" is not defined. Presumably it is limited to officials representing the government in some capacity, similar to "covered U.S. persons" as defined in §7432(4).

[63] 22 U.S.C. § 7426(e).

[64] 22 U.S.C. § 7430.

[65] 22 U.S.C. § 7430(a).

[66] 22 U.S.C. § 7431. It is unclear what authority is meant with respect to section 2011(a) (22 U.S.C. § 7430(a)), since section 2011 does not vest any authority in the President. *See* 22 U.S.C. § 7430(c). Perhaps section 2012 should be interpreted to prohibit delegation of the authorities to which sections 2004 and 2006 do not apply under section 2011.

[67] Section 2004 (22 U.S.C. § 7423) restricts the conduct of federal and state agencies and courts. Therefore, the exception in section 2011 could not be invoked with respect to state courts and other non-federal entities. Section 2006 (22 U.S.C. § 7425) applies only to the President, directing him to implement procedures to safeguard certain information from the ICC; a broad interpretation of section 2011 would appear to render section 2006 a nullity. Perhaps section 2011 is meant to provide the President authority to suspend regulations promulgated under section 2006 with respect to certain cases under the jurisdiction of the ICC.

[68] 22 U.S.C. § 7433(a).

[69] 22 U.S.C. § 7428. No such report was made public, but the report may have been submitted in classified form pursuant to subsection (c).

[70] Id.

[71] S. REP. NO. 109-277 (2006).

[72] H. REP. NO. 109-452, at 389-90 (2006). The Committee praised IMET programs, stating that such programs create opportunities for military-to-military engagement between U.S. armed forces and the militaries of developing nations. Such interactions are critical to advancing the understanding of, and respect for, civil-military relations; enhancing the understanding of U.S. military principles and values; bridging cultural differences; and developing important long-term relationships with future military and civilian leaders. Generally, such engagement has positively affected U.S. armed forces' global access and influence and has proved helpful in the global war on terrorism.

[73] *See* Grossman, *supra* note 12.

[74] 18 U.S.C. § 2441.

[75] Genocide Convention Implementation Act of 1987, P.L. 100-606, 102 Stat. 3045 (codified at 18 U.S.C. §§ 1091-93).

[76] See Douglass Cassel, Empowering United States Courts to Hear Crimes Within the Jurisdiction of the International Court, 35 NEW ENG. L. REV. 421, 437 (2001); Robinson O. Everett, American Servicemembers and the ICC, in THE UNITED STATES AND THE INTERNATIONAL CRIMINAL COURT 137, 142 (Sarah B. Sewall and Carl Kaysen, eds. 2000).

[77] See Douglass Cassel, Empowering United States Courts to Hear Crimes Within the Jurisdiction of the International Court, 35 NEW ENG. L. REV. 421, 429 (2001).

[78] *See id.* n.39 (listing relevant crimes over which U.S. courts have extraterritorial jurisdiction). Additionally, U.S. courts have jurisdiction to try criminal offenses committed by persons employed by or accompanying the armed forces overseas, or ex-servicemembers who committed a crime overseas, if such crime would be punishable by imprisonment for more than one year if it had committed within the territorial jurisdiction of the United States. 18 U.S.C. § 3261.

[79] Rome Statute, *supra* note 2, art. 123.

[80] *Id.* art. 23.

[81] *Id.* arts. 112 and 123. States that have signed the Statute or the Final Act are eligible to participate as observers in both bodies. The Administration's notification of intent not to ratify the Statute should have no effect on eligibility, although it may signal an intent not to participate. The United States did not participate at the final meeting of the Preparatory Commission in early July, possibly signaling the intent of the Administration to forego participation as an observer.

[82] *See* Assembly of States Parties to the Rome Statute of the International Criminal Court, First Session, Official Records, U.N. Doc ICC ASP/1/3 (2003). The Rules of Procedure of the Assembly of States Parties ["Assembly Rules"] are reprinted in part IIC of the conference report.

[83] Unlike the previous administration, the Bush Administration did not participate actively in Preparatory Commission meetings, suggesting that the Administration does not envision playing an active role as observer at the Assembly of States Parties.

[84] The United Nations has a standing invitation to participate as an observer. Assembly Rule 35. It may also propose items for the agenda. Assembly Rule 11. Finally, the U.N. may provide funding for the ICC, in particular

with respect to cases referred by the Security Council. Rome Statute, *supra* note 2, art. 115; *see also* U.N. Doc., PCNICC/2001/1/Add. 1, Draft Relationship Agreement between the Court and the United Nations.

[85] Rome Statute, *supra* note 2, art. 13. Non-parties might also be able to provide information to enable the Prosecutor to initiate a self-referred investigation, but would have no *official* role in advocating prosecution.

[86] *Id.* art. 16.

[87] *Id.* art. 53.

[88] *Id.* arts. 86, 87, and 93.

[89] *Id.* arts. 59 and 89.

[90] *Id.* art. 72.

[91] *Id.* art. 73.

[92] *Id.* art. 115.

[93] *See* Lee A. Casey, *The Case Against the International Criminal Court*, 25 FORDHAM INT'L L.J. 840, 849-50 (2002).

[94] *See* Final Report to the Prosecutor by the Committee Established to Review the NATO Bombing Campaign Against the Federal Republic of Yugoslavia, *available at* [http://www.un.org/icty/pressreal/nato06 1 300.htm](last visited June 14, 2006).

[95] *See, e.g.*, Leila Nadya Sadat and S. Richard Carden, *The New International Criminal Court: An Uneasy Revolution,* 88 GEO. L.J. 381, 392 (2000) (suggesting that the refusal of the United States to participate in the ICC could bring about its demise, just as the U.S.' failure to join the League of Nations contributed to the failure of that institution).

[96] *See* Major Eric S. Kraus and Major Mike O. Lacy, *Utilitarian vs. Humanitarian: The Battle over the Law of War*, PARAMETERS, Jul. 1, 2002, *available at* 2002 WL 18222339. (commenting that U.S. refusal to ratify Protocol I to the Geneva Conventions, the treaty banning antipersonnel landmines, and the Rome Statute appear to be diminishing U.S. influence on the development of customary international law).

[97] An example might be the impact the U.S. policy has had on U.S. relations with Europe. *See* CRS Report RS21612, *East Central Europe: Status of International Criminal Court (ICC) Exemption Agreements and U.S. Military Assistance*, by Julie Kim.

[98] *The International Criminal Court: Hearing Before the House Committee on International Relations*, 106th Cong. 4 (2000) (prepared testimony of John Bolton, Senior Vice President, American Enterprise Institute).

[99] *See supra* note 50.

[100] SC Res. 1422, U.N. Doc. S/Res/1422 (2002), *available at* [http://daccessdds.un.org].

[101] SC Res. 1497, U.N. Doc. S/RES/1497, Para. 7 (Aug. 1, 2003).

[102] Certification Concerning U.S. Participation in the U.N. Mission in Liberia Consistent With Section 2005 of the American Servicemembers' Protection Act, 68 Fed. Reg. 63,975 (2003).

[103] SC Res. 1529, U.N. Doc. S/RES/1529 (2004) (authorizing multinational interim force to deploy to Haiti).

[104] SC Res. 1542, U.N. Doc. S/RES/1542 (2004).

[105] 69 Fed. Reg. 34,043 (June 14, 2004).

[106] *See* "Security Council Refers Situation in Darfur, Sudan, to Prosecutor of International Criminal Court," Press Release, SC/8351; "Secretary-General Welcomes Adoption of Security Council Resolution Referring Situation in Darfur, Sudan to International Criminal Court Prosecutor," March 31, 2005, Press Release SG/SM/9797 AFR/1132. For background, see "Report of the International Commission of Inquiry on Darfur to the United Nations Secretary-General," S/2005/60, January 25, 2005

[107] *See* "U.N. Commission's Report on Violations of International Humanitarian Law in Darfur: Security Council Referral to the International Criminal Court," Frederic L. Kirgis, Am. Soc'y Int'l L Insight (Addendum), April 5, 2005.

[108] United Nations Security Council Resolution 1593 was adopted by the Security Council at its 518th meeting on 31 March 2005, U.N. Doc. S/RES/1593 (2005).

[109] *See* SC Res. 1564, U.N. Doc. S.RES/1564(2004) (requesting the establishment of an International Commission of Inquiry).

[110] *See* SC Res. 1593, Para. 6; *see also* Kirgis, *supra* note 107.

[111] *See* Jess Bravin, *U.S. Warms To Hague Tribunal*, WALL ST. J., June 14, 2006, at A4.

[112] United States Mission to the United Nations, "Statement on the Sudan Accountability Resolution," Ambassador Anne W. Patterson, March 31, 2005. *See* CRS Report RL33574, *Sudan: Humanitarian Crisis, Peace Talks, Terrorism, and U.S. Policy*, by Ted Dagne.

[113] *See* DOS Press Release, *supra* note 59. For the text of one such agreement, see Agreement Between the Government of the United States of America and the Republic of Uzbekistan Regarding the Surrender of Persons to the International Criminal Court, September 18, 2002, T.I.A.S. No. _____, *reprinted in* 42 I.L.M. 39 (2003).

[114] Rome Statute, *supra* note 2, art. 98.

[115] Risks for the Integrity of the Statute of the International Criminal Court, Resolution 1300 of the Parliamentary Assembly of the Council of Europe (September 25, 2002).

[116] *See* Phillip Shiskin and Jesse Bravin, *EU Offers Deal on U.S. Immunity from Tribunal*, WALL ST. J., Sep. 13, 2002, at A8.

[117] *See* Council of the European Union: Council Conclusions and EU Guiding Principles, 42 I.L.M. 240 (2003); *see also* Council of the European Union, Threats to the International Criminal Court, Resolution 1336 (2003).

[118] Press Release, Council of the European Union, 15864/1/04 REV 1 (Presse 353) P 136/04, Dec. 10, 2004.

[119] *See, e.g.* Coalition for the International Criminal Court, Overview of the United States' Opposition to the International Criminal Court (Nov. 1, 2005), *available at* [http://www.iccnow.org/documents/CICCFS_US%20Opposition%20toICC_FINAL_eng% 20_2_.pdf] (last visited June 14, 2006); Human Rights Watch, United States Efforts to Undermine the International Criminal Court, (Sep. 4, 2002), *available at* [http://hrw.org/campaigns/icc/docs/art98analysis.htm](last visited June 14, 2006).

[120] Relevant U.N. Security Council Resolutions are S/RES/1386 (2001), S/RES/14 13 (2002), S/RES/1444 (2002, S/RES/1510 (2003), S/RES/1563 (2004), and S/RES/1623 (2005). None of these resolutions makes provisions regarding immunity for participating troops.

[121] *See* Colum Lynch, *Deal Gave Europe's Troops Immunity*, INT'L HERALD TRIB., June 20, 2002, at A1. Section 1.4 of Annex A to the MTA provides: The ISAF and supporting personnel, including associated liaison personnel, will be immune from personal arrest or detention. ISAF and supporting personnel, including associated liaison personnel, mistakenly arrested or detained will be immediately handed over to ISAF authorities. The Interim Administration agree that ISAF and supporting personnel, including associated liaison personnel, may not be surrendered to, or otherwise transferred to the custody of, an international tribunal or any other entity or State without the express consent of the contributing nation. ISAF Forces will respect the laws and culture of Afghanistan. The text of the agreement may be downloaded from the U.K. ISAF website at [http://www.operations.mod.uk/isafmta.doc](last visited June 14, 2006).

[122] *See* Rome Statute, *supra* note 2, arts. 97 & 98.

[123] *Id.* art. 5(1).

In: International Criminal Court
Editor: Harry P. Milton, pp. 79-138

ISBN: 978-1-60692-723-6
© 2009 Nova Science Publishers, Inc.

Chapter 3

INTERNATIONAL CRIMINAL COURT: OVERVIEW AND SELECTED LEGAL ISSUES

Jennifer Elsea

PREFACE

The International Criminal Court (ICC) is the first global permanent international court with jurisdiction to prosecute individuals for "the most serious crimes of concern to the international community." The United Nations, many human rights organizations, and most democratic nations have expressed support for the new court. The Bush Administration firmly opposes it and has formally renounced the U.S. obligations under the treaty. At the same time, however, the Administration has stressed that the United States shares the goals of the ICC's supporters-promotion of the rule of law-and does not intend to take any action to undermine the ICC.

The primary objection given by the U.S. in opposition to the treaty is the ICC's possible assertion of the jurisdiction over U.S. soldiers charged with "war crimes" resulting from legitimate uses of force. The main issue faced by the current Congress is whether to adopt a policy aimed at preventing the ICC from becoming effective or whether to continue contributing to the development of the ICC in order to improve it.

This book provides a historical background of the negotiations for the Rome Statute, outlines the structure of the International Criminal Court (ICC) as contained in the final Statute, and describes the jurisdiction of the ICC. The book further identifies the specific crimes enumerated in the Rome Statute as supplemented by the draft elements of crime. A discussion of procedural safeguards follows, including reference to the draft procedural rules.

The book then goes on to discuss the implications for the United States as a non-ratifying country when the ICC comes into being, and outlines some legislation enacted and proposed to regulate U.S relations with the ICC.

INTRODUCTION AND NEGOTIATING HISTORY

On April 11, 2002, the Rome Statute of the International Criminal Court[1] received its sixtieth ratification, meaning it will come into effect July 1, 2002, years earlier than had been predicted. The ICC will be the first global permanent international court with jurisdiction to prosecute individuals for "the most serious crimes of concern to the international community;"[2] the United Nations, many human rights organizations, and most democratic nations have expressed support for the new court.[3] The Bush Administration, however, firmly opposes it and has taken the measure of formally renouncing any U.S. obligations under the treaty.[4] Some critics have remarked that the issue is causing a rift between the United States and its allies in the war against terrorism.[5] At the same time, the Administration has stressed that the United States shares the goal of the ICC's supporters - promotion of the rule of law - and does not intend to take any action to undermine the ICC.[6] In a move that may foreshadow the Administration's strategy, the United States is also reportedly seeking assurances from the United Nations that no U.N. personnel taking part in the peacekeeping mission in East Timor will be subject to prosecution by any local or international court for war crimes - a move that has met with resistance from U.S. allies because they say it could undermine the principles of the ICC.[7]

While the United States initially supported the idea of creating an international criminal court[8] and was a major participant at the Rome Conference,[9] in the end, the United States - joined by Iran, Iraq, China, Israel, Sudan, and Libya - voted against the Statute.[10] Nevertheless, President Clinton signed the treaty December 31, 2000 - the last day it was open for signature without simultaneous ratification, at the same time declaring that the treaty contained "significant flaws" and that he would not submit it to the Senate for its advice and consent "until our fundamental concerns are satisfied."[11] The Bush Administration has likewise declined to submit the Rome Statute to the Senate for ratification, and has notified the depositary of the United Nations of the U.S.

intent not to ratify the treaty.[12] The primary objection given by the United States in opposition to the treaty is the ICC's possible assertion of jurisdiction over U.S. soldiers charged with "war crimes" resulting from legitimate uses of force, even if the United States does not ratify the Rome Statute. The United States sought to exempt U.S. soldiers and employees from the jurisdiction of the ICC based on the unique position the United States occupies with regard to international peacekeeping.[13] The main issue faced by the Congress is the level of cooperation to allow between the United States and the ICC: to withhold all cooperation from the ICC and its member nations in order to prevent the ICC from becoming effective, to continue contributing to the development of the ICC in order to improve it, or to adopt a pragmatic approach based solely on U.S. interests.[14]

This report provides an historical background of the negotiations for the Rome Statute, outlines the structure of the ICC as contained in the final Statute, and describes the jurisdiction of the ICC. The report identifies the specific crimes enumerated in the Rome Statute as supplemented by the draft elements of crime drawn up by the Preparatory Commission established by the Rome Conference. A discussion of procedural safeguards follows, including reference to the draft procedural rules. The report then discusses the implications for the United States, as a non-ratifying country as the ICC comes into being, and outlines some legislation enacted and proposed to regulate U.S. relations with the ICC.

The creation of the ICC is the culmination of a decades-long effort to establish an international court with the jurisdiction to try individuals for the commission of crimes against humanity.[15] The post-World War II tribunals to try Nazi and Japanese war criminals established precedent for the ICC. The later International Criminal Tribunal for Yugoslavia (ICTY) and the International Criminal Tribunal for Rwanda (ICTR) built upon the Nuremberg legacy. However, all of these courts were created *ad hoc* with limited jurisdiction. An international court with jurisdiction over all crimes of the worst nature affecting mankind was urged in order to end impunity for *any and all* perpetrators of large-scale atrocities. The U.N. General Assembly voted to establish an Ad Hoc Committee on the Establishment of an International Criminal Court[16] and created a Preparatory Committee charged with "preparing a widely acceptable consolidated text of a convention for an International Criminal Court as a next step towards consideration by a conference of plenipotentiaries."[17]

The Preparatory Committee held six sessions between March 1996 and April 1998 to prepare a text for consideration at the Rome Conference.[18] The most contentious issue at the Conference revolved around the level of independence the ICC would have vis-a-vis national courts and the U.N. Security Council. The

Preparatory Commission considered two basic options for defining the jurisdiction of the ICC: The ICC might assert jurisdiction over all relevant crimes, exercising primacy over national courts, without regard to the nationality of the victims or perpetrators. Under this option, "rogue" regimes would be unable to insulate themselves from responsibility for crimes committed against opposing forces or ethnic minorities, even during internal armed conflicts. Many countries, including the United States, objected to the idea as an intrusion into the sovereignty of nations. Second, the ICC's power to try cases could be "complementary" to that of national courts, where the ICC would exercise jurisdiction only when national courts of the country in which the crime took place, or whose national was accused, were unable or unwilling to prosecute. The second model, which the United States had supported, was adopted in principle.[19]

The adoption of the complementarity model of jurisdiction led to the even more intractable question of how and when the ICC would take a case. Possible options included a recommendation by the U.N. Security Council, a recommendation by a country with personal or subject matter jurisdiction over the crime or the accused, or upon the initiative of the ICC itself. Taking the position that treaty regimes should apply only to those states that choose to become parties and not to those that choose to remain outside, the United States delegation offered amendments at Rome to require the consent of both the State in which the crime was allegedly committed and of the state of nationality of the alleged perpetrator, or, failing that, at least of the state of nationality, to the jurisdiction of the Court.[20] Under the U.S. proposals, the ICC would have jurisdiction over citizens of non-consenting non-parties only in cases referred or authorized by the U.N. Security Council, which would have allowed the United States and other permanent members of the Council to veto any attempt to prosecute their citizens, but would allow for the prosecution of state architects of genocidal policies, for example, as long as the political support could be generated in the Security Council.

The conferees rejected this proposal on the grounds that it would essentially mirror the present application of *ad hoc* tribunals, bringing some perpetrators of crimes against humanity to justice while allowing others to escape with impunity.[21] Additionally, in their view, a treaty that subjects citizens of non-parties to an international court's jurisdiction does not bind the non-party state to *do* anything and thus does not infringe on its sovereignty.[22] Aliens who commit crimes are subject to the jurisdiction of local courts in any event. Under this view, assuming that the referring state would have the jurisdiction to try or extradite an alien accused of a crime on its territory, the referring state could just as legitimately cede its jurisdiction over the accused to an international court.[23]

The U.S. delegation also proposed to exempt from the Court's jurisdiction conduct that arises from the official actions of a non-party state acknowledged as such by the non-party. The United States, it was argued, would willingly acknowledge the official nature of conduct related to peacekeeping missions or other foreign affairs activity and thus gain an exemption from the Court's jurisdiction for alleged crimes arising from such missions.[24] This, it proposed, would eliminate the disincentive for non-party States to participate in peacekeeping missions. Dictators, it said, would be reluctant to admit responsibility for conduct that could be viewed as criminal under the Rome Statute. The conference voted to take no action on the proposal.[25] The final rule allows the ICC to take a case on the recommendation of one of the countries with the appropriate jurisdiction, the U.N. Security Council, or the ICC Prosecutor.

The U.S. delegation to Rome, led by David Scheffer, then Ambassador-at-Large for War Crimes Issues, argued that allowing the Prosecutor-to initiate cases would potentially put U.S. military personnel in jeopardy of being summoned in front of the ICC on groundless charges. The United States is in a unique position in the world, Scheffer argued, in which it is frequently called upon to respond to international crises, often by deploying U.S. troops and government officials to hostile countries. If those countries could retaliate by accusing the United States and its officials or military personnel of war crimes, for example, the United States could find itself hamstrung in its peacekeeping efforts. The Rome delegates adopted four methods to accommodate U.S. concerns regarding abuse of prosecutorial discretion: limiting the power of the ICC Prosecutor, requiring the consent of a country which would have jurisdiction over an alleged crime before initiating a prosecution, narrowly defining the crimes for which a person may be prosecuted, and creating a role for the U.N. Security Council,[26] though not adopting the U.S. suggestion which would have allowed any permanent member of the Security Council to veto any proposed prosecution.

Instead, the Rome Conference adopted the so-called Singapore Proposal, which, rather than requiring unanimity of the permanent members of the Security Council to initiate a prosecution, would require unanimity in order to block prosecution temporarily.[27] Because the Permanent Five would have to cooperate in order to authorize a peace-keeping mission in the first place, it was reasoned, all five could be expected to agree to block any unwarranted ICC prosecutions that might arise.[28] This proposal would not guarantee immunity in the case of a unilateral action on the part of the United States, however, and failed to gain the support of the U.S. delegation.

Although the United States voted against the Rome Statute to establish an ICC, it did sign the Final Act of the Conference.[29] As a consequence, it was able to participate as a voting member of the Preparatory Commission created by the Rome conference. The Preparatory Commission has developed draft rules of procedure and evidence, the elements of crimes, a relationship agreement between the ICC and the U.N., financial regulations, an agreement on privileges and immunities, a budget, and the rules of procedure to govern the Assembly of States Parties.[30] It has not yet completed its work on the definition of the crime of aggression.

STRUCTURE OF THE ICC

The Rome Statute establishes the Court's structure and provides rules for its limited governance by the states parties to the Statute. The ICC will consist of the Presidency, three Trial Divisions, the Office of the Prosecutor, and the Registry.[31] It will have international legal personality to carry out its functions,[32] and its relationship to the United Nations will be established by agreement between the ICC president and the U.N.[33]

The Rome Statute is designed to provide for the independence of the prosecutor and judges. However, it also provides a system of checks and balances designed to rein in overzealous prosecutors and prevent the ICC from falling under the control of biased judges or states with an interest in the outcome. For example, for a prosecutor to initiate a case, he must first get independent authorization from the ICC's Pre-Trial Chamber to continue an investigation.[34] The statute's requirements for election of judges are designed to diminish the possibility that the pre-trial chamber would be politicized, thereby increasing its ability to prevent prosecutors from bringing unwarranted charges. The candidates for judge are required to be competent in either criminal law or in relevant areas of international law,[35] and no two judges are permitted to be from the same state.[36] The person being investigated may request the disqualification of any judge when the judge's "impartiality might reasonably be doubted."[37] The trial and appellate chambers are kept separate to enable parties to challenge both interlocutory and final decisions before different judges. Finally, it provides mechanisms for checks by majority vote of the Assembly of States Parties, a representative body of the member states.

The Judges of the ICC: The Presidencyand Trial Divisions

A total of eighteen judges will be elected to serve staggered nine-year terms on the ICC, subject to a possible increase in the number of judges upon recommendation by the President and its approval by the Assembly of States Parties. States parties to the ICC may nominate one qualified candidate for each election. Judicial candidates must be nationals of states parties to the Rome Statute, although not necessarily of the nominating state.[38] The Assembly of States Parties may establish an advisory committee on nominations as it deems appropriate.[39] Judges will be selected by vote of the Assembly of States Parties to be representative of the world's population in terms of legal systems, geography, legal specialties, and gender.[40] Judges will not be permitted to pursue outside occupations, and may be removed from office by a vote of two-thirds majority of the Assembly of States Parties to affirm a recommendation by two-thirds of the other judges that the judge be removed for serious misconduct or inability to carry out the functions of the position.[41]

The Presidency consists of a President and two Vice-Presidents, who are to be elected from the judge corps by an absolute majority of its members.[42] The President and Vice Presidents serve for three-year terms, unless their terms as judges expire earlier, with one opportunity for re-election. The President will have overall responsibility for the administration of the Court (with the exception of the Office of the Prosecutor) and for other functions, such as deciding which judges will hear which cases and whether to excuse a particular judge or prosecutor from any particular case for reasons of possible conflict of interest.

The 18 judges will be divided among the Pre-Trial Division, Trial Division, and Appeals Division. Judges assigned to the Appeals Division remain there throughout their tenure, while judges initially assigned to the Trial or Pre-Trial Divisions serve three-year terms plus any time necessary to complete ongoing hearings. Judges assigned to the Trial or Pre-Trial Divisions may be temporarily shifted between the two divisions to accommodate the workload of the ICC, but judges assigned to the Appeals Division, which will include the President, may not be temporarily assigned to another division.[43]

The Pre-Trial Division, by majority vote of a three-judge chamber, decides issues regarding admissibility of evidence and jurisdiction of the Court to hear a case, authorizes the prosecutor to pursue self-initiated investigations, determines whether sufficient evidence exists to support an indictment, and issues rulings regarding the withholding of material held by a state that deems the disclosure of such information to be prejudicial to the national security of that state.[44] Other issues may be decided by individual judges, including rulings necessary to ensure privacy and security of witnesses and actions to seek the cooperation of a state in executing one of the majority-issued orders.

The Trial Division consists of two chambers of three judges each and is responsible for the fair and expeditious conduct of trials with proper regard for the rights of the accused and security of witnesses. The Trial Chambers have the authority to decide intermediary issues by majority decision or to refer such issues to the Pre-Trial Division. They are responsible for confirming that the accused understands the nature of the charges and that pleas are voluntary, and for providing an accurate transcript of 'the proceedings.' The Trial Division also sentences the accused upon conviction, based on all relevant evidence supplemented by means of additional hearings, when necessary.[45]

The Appeals Division consists of a single chamber of five judges, including the ICC President, that hears appeals of convictions, sentences, and acquittals, as well as interlocutory rulings on admissibility of evidence, jurisdiction, and the like. The Appeals Chamber has powers comparable to those of the Trial Division, and may reverse or amend a decision or sentence, or it may order a new trial before a different chamber.[46] A convicted person or his survivors or designee may bring an appeal any time new evidence becomes available that could have changed the outcome of a case.

The Appeals Division may reject such an application it determines to be unfounded, or it may order new proceedings before the original or a new Trial Chamber, or retain jurisdiction over the matter.[47] In cases of grave and manifest miscarriages of justice, it may award compensation to an arrested or convicted person.[48]

Prosecutor

The Prosecutor is selected by an absolute majority of the Assembly of States Parties via secret ballot.[49] The Assembly then votes, again in secret, to select Deputy Prosecutors from a list of candidates provided by the Prosecutor. The Prosecutor and Deputy Prosecutors are each eligible to hold office for one nine-year term, without the possibility of re-election. During their terms in office, they may not engage in any activities that might place their impartiality in doubt, and any of them may be disqualified from a particular case by the Appeals Chamber if the person being investigated or prosecuted so requests. If it is found that the Prosecutor has committed serious misconduct, breached his or her duties, or is no longer able to carry out his or her functions under the Statute, an absolute majority of the Assembly may decide by secret ballot to disqualify him or her. A Deputy

Prosecutor may be removed for like reasons by an absolute majority of the Assembly upon the recommendation of the Prosecutor. In either proceeding, the Prosecutor or Deputy Prosecutor is allowed to present and receive evidence in order to dispute the charges.

The Office of the Prosecutor receives referrals from the U.N. Security Council and member states on possible crimes within the jurisdiction of the Court for investigation to determine whether prosecution is warranted. The Rome Statute also allows investigations to be initiated by the Prosecutor, subject to approval by the majority of a Pre-Trial Chamber. The Prosecutor determines whether the information available establishes a reasonable basis to conduct an investigation.[50] If there is such a basis, the Prosecutor shall "extend the investigation to cover all facts and evidence relevant to an assessment of whether there is criminal responsibility under [the Rome] Statute," giving equal consideration to exonerating evidence as is given to incriminating information, and taking care to respect the interests of victims and witnesses, as well as the rights of the accused.[51] The Prosecutor may conduct investigations on the territory of a state that is a party to the Statute or agrees to cooperate.[52]

The role of the ICC Prosecutor remains a point of contention for the United States, which sought more limits on the power of the Prosecutor to launch cases on his own initiative. The U.S. opposed granting this discretion to the Prosecutor on the grounds it would "encourage overwhelming the Court with complaints and risk diversion of its resources, as well as embroil the Court in controversy, political decision making, and confusion."[53]

Registry

The Office of the Registry is responsible under the Rome Statute for the non-judicial administration of the Court,[54] including providing for witness protection and assistance, as well as for receiving prisoners, arranging for the defense of indigents, and surrendering convicted persons to the state of incarceration. The Registrar, who will head the Registry as the chief administrative officer of the Court, is elected by an absolute majority of the judges by secret ballot after considering the Assembly's recommendations. The Registrar serves on a full-time basis for up to two five-year terms. Deputy registrars may serve shorter terms and need not serve full-time.

As part of its duties with regard to witnesses, the Registrar is responsible for the creation of the Victims and Witnesses Unit (VWU), which will be charged with recommending and providing protection, counseling, and assistance to witnesses and victims who appear before the Court, as well as others who may be placed at risk due to testimony given by other witnesses, in order to prevent their suffering mental or physical violence.[55] VWU staff must have expertise in treating trauma victims, including children and victims of sex crimes and violence.

The Rome Statute does not provide for a separate unit within the Registry to provide its mandated support to the defense.[56] However, draft Rules of Procedure and Evidence, Rule 20[57] requires the Registrar to organize the staff of the Registry "in a manner that promotes the rights of the defense, consistent with the principle of fair trial," and to perform certain duties in order to ensure the independence of defense counsel, providing the defense with support, facilities, and information; helping the accused to obtain the assistance of competent legal counsel;[58] and cooperating with state defense and bar associations. The Registrar is responsible for drafting a list of criteria for assigning defense counsel[59] and a code of professional responsibility for all counsel.[60]

Assembly of States Parties

The Assembly of States Parties is not an organ of the ICC, but is comprised of a representative of each ratifying state, with each state having one vote.[61] Non-party states who have signed the Rome Statute or its Final Act may participate as observers but may not vote. The Assembly provides management and oversight to the Presidency, the Prosecutor, and the Registrar regarding the administration of the ICC, including the budget, the number of judges, and rules of procedure and evidence. The Assembly also makes determinations in the event a state party fails to comply with a request to cooperate, or refers the matter to the U.N. Security Council if the case was referred to the ICC by that body. The Assembly also elects 21 persons to serve three-year terms as members of the Bureau, and it may establish other subsidiary bodies to carry out oversight functions.

The Assembly of States Parties may amend the Rome Statute in accordance with art. 121. After seven years have passed since the Statute has entered into force, any state party may propose an amendment, which will be adopted if a two-thirds majority of the Assembly of States Parties votes in its favor. Amendments enter into force for all states parties one year after seven-eighths of the states parties have deposited their instruments of ratification or acceptance with the U.N. Secretary-General. Any state party which has not accepted the amendment may withdraw from the Statute with immediate effect by giving notice within one year after its entry into force.

Critics of the Rome Statute question the future ability of the Assembly of States Parties to exercise any real accountability over the operations of the ICC.[62] They predict that the one-vote-per-state rule could lend lopsided sway to tiny countries,[63] and complain that the Statute does not provide for the democratic accountability of a state's representative at the Assembly to the citizens of the state. Critics also note that representatives will be able to vote at the Assembly and influence the development of the ICC even though they may represent non-democratic countries with poor human rights records or who are proclaimed adversaries of the United States.[64]

JURISDICTION

Subject Matter Jurisdiction

Article 5 of the final Statute limits the jurisdiction of the ICC to the "most serious crimes of concern to the international community as a whole," namely, genocide, crimes against humanity, war crimes and, potentially, aggression and terrorism.[65] Article 8 of the final Statute limits the ICC's jurisdiction over "war crimes" primarily to those committed as "part of a plan or policy or as part of a large-scale commission of such crimes."[66]

The ICC's jurisdiction will extend only to crimes committed after its inception. However, the Statute allows states parties to the Statute to opt out of the ICC's jurisdiction over war crimes for a period of seven years after becoming a party, as well as its jurisdiction over any new crimes that may be added to the Statute in the future.[67] The United States had wanted an initial opt-out provision that would have allowed states parties to assess the effectiveness and impartiality of the Court for a longer period of time with respect to all of the covered crimes before deciding whether to submit to the full jurisdiction of the Court. However, the proposal was rejected, as was a U.S. proposal allowing non-states parties to opt out (or in) for the ICC's jurisdiction over specific crimes. Thus, the ICC appears initially to have broader jurisdiction over war crimes allegedly committed by citizens of non-member states than it will have over war crimes allegedly committed by citizens of states that ratify the treaty.[68]

The elements of each of the crimes, drafted largely at the insistence of the U.S. negotiating team,[69] will likely be adopted once the ICC comes into existence and should serve to check the discretion of the ICC judges and prosecutor.[70] The draft elements may also help to resolve any possible problems caused by vagueness, inherent in international treaties due to the perceived elevated importance of compromise over clarity, but seen as detrimental to fairness in enforcing criminal law, which requires specificity.[71] The Rome Statute provides for amendment of the elements of crimes by two-thirds vote of the Assembly of State Parties. The crimes and their draft elements are summarized below.

Genocide

The Preparatory Committee borrowed the language regarding the crime of genocide used in the 1948 Genocide Convention,[72] which prohibits a number of acts when carried out "with intent to destroy, in whole or in part, a national, ethnical, racial or religious group, as such,"[73] whether carried out in war or during peacetime. The definition is virtually identical to that adopted by Congress in the Genocide Convention Implementation Act of 1987, except that the U.S. Code covers only conduct committed by a U.S. national or conduct committed within the United States.[74]

The victim of genocide is not the individual but the group itself, membership in which is determined automatically by birth rather than by individual choice.[75] The aim must be physical destruction and not merely "cultural genocide," or eliminating the cultural attributes of specific groups, for example, through forced assimilation.[76] To make out a case for genocide, the prosecutor must show that the victim or victims were members of a particular national, ethnic, racial or religious group; the perpetrator intended to destroy that group in whole or in part; and that the perpetrator's conduct (which might include failure to take certain actions[77]) took place in the context of a manifest pattern of similar conduct directed against that group or was conduct that could itself effect such destruction.[78] It is the *mens rea* element that separates genocide from other crimes against humanity: the intent to destroy a group of people as a whole or in significant part.[79]

Crimes Against Humanity

The London Charter creating the Nuremberg tribunal was the first codification of the prohibition using the term "crimes against humanity," although the drafters did not treat it as a new concept.[70] There exists no treaty requiring states to prosecute crimes against humanity, but there is universal jurisdiction under customary international law to punish as *hostis humani generis* - enemies of mankind - without regard to territorial jurisdiction over a crime or criminal.[81] These crimes include universally condemned acts such as murder, extermination, enslavement, deportation, or religious or political persecution, when carried out as part of a widespread or systematic attack against a civilian population.[82] The distinction between these crimes and war crimes is that they may occur during war or peace and may be perpetrated against stateless victims and persons of the perpetrator's own nationality or that of an allied state.[83] Random crimes would not amount to crimes against humanity; "widespread or systematic" plan or policy does not necessarily connote an intent to destroy a group of people in whole or in part.

The last two elements for each of the crimes against humanity clarify the requisite participation in and knowledge of the systematic plan or attack, but are not intended to be interpreted as requiring proof that the perpetrator had knowledge of all characteristics of the attack or the precise details of the plan or policy of the state or organization.[84] The mental element is satisfied in the case of an emerging attack if the perpetrator intended to further such an attack by any means. The acts need not constitute a military attack. An act perpetrated without constructive or actual knowledge of the existence of the widespread policy or plan would lack the *mens rea* for a crime against humanity. Motive is not relevant.[85]

Although there is no U.S. statute codifying crimes against humanity as such, U.S. criminal law prohibits most of the crimes enumerated under the Rome Statute as possible crimes against humanity, as long as they are committed within the United States or by military personnel.[86] Under current law, acts that could constitute crimes against humanity committed by U.S. civilians overseas generally are not triable in U.S. civil or military courts unless they involve torture or certain acts of international terrorism.[87]

War Crimes

War crimes are violations of the international law of war committed during an armed conflict or military occupation,[88] whenever a belligerent "crosses the line" with respect to acceptable combat practices.[89] The Rome statute defines war crimes in art. 8, reiterating war crimes as they are defined in detail in the of Geneva[90] and Hague Conventions,[91] with emphasis on those crimes committed as part of a plan or policy or as part of a large-scale commission of such crimes.[92] States that are parties to the treaty have the right under Article 124 to opt out of the ICC's jurisdiction with respect to war crimes for a period of seven years.

The prosecutor must show that the crimes took place in the context of an armed conflict, that the perpetrator was aware of those circumstances, and that the perpetrator was aware that the victim had protected status under the Geneva Conventions or Protocols.[93] There is no need to show that the act was committed as part of a widespread series of violations.[94]

The War Crimes Act of 1996[95] establishes U.S. federal jurisdiction to punish war crimes, as defined in international treaties to which the United States is a party, when perpetrated by or against U.S. nationals. U.S. service members and others may also be tried by courts-martial or military commission for acts in violation of the law of war;[96] ordinarily, U.S. practice is to try U.S. service members by court-martial rather than in federal court for offenses against the law of war.[97]

Aggression

The Rome Conference Delegates included "aggression" among the crimes over which the ICC would have jurisdiction, but were unable to reach an agreement to adopt a definition.[98] Instead, the Conferees agreed to work toward establishing a definition after the Rome Statute enters into force. The ICC will be able to exercise jurisdiction over the crime of aggression only after such a provision has been adopted and entered into force for the relevant state party.

Although there were trials for aggression at Nuremberg,[99] an acceptable definition for its elements has long eluded the international community, impeding earlier attempts to establish an international criminal court.[100] Article 39 of the U.N. Charter leaves it to the Security Council to determine the existence of and take action with respect to "any threat to the peace, breach of the peace, or act of aggression."[101] Aggression is not defined in the U.N. Charter, however, because it was reportedly feared that advances in weapons and techniques of modern warfare would make the definition impractical and subject to manipulation, and might cause the Security Council to take premature action.[102] The U.N. General Assembly adopted a resolution in 1974[103] addressing the definition of aggression, but it has only been invoked once by the Security Council, to declare South Mica guilty of aggression against Angola.[104] The definition contains an enumeration of offenses included as possible aggression, but leaves the determination to the Security Council.[105]

· Any definition of aggression adopted for the ICC must "be consistent with the relevant provisions of the Charter of the United Nations."[106] If this provision is interpreted to include a determination by the Security Council that an act of aggression has been committed in the definition for aggression under the Rome Statute, then the United States and NATO likely need not fear prosecution for acts of aggression.[107] On the other hand, some observers have expressed concern that the Rome Statute can be used to divest the Security Council of its prerogative in determining whether an act of aggression has occurred, allowing legitimate acts of self-defense to be punished as aggression.[108] Such a result could, they argue, curtail the U.S.' options for using military force for valid reasons.

Jurisdiction over Persons

It is widely accepted that the above crimes enumerated in the Statute are subject to universal jurisdiction under international law;[109] that is, any nation may lawfully try any individual accused of such crimes in its domestic court system without regard to the nationality of the alleged perpetrator or the territory where the crime is alleged to have taken place.[110] In practice, however, political realities appear often to have precluded nations from asserting jurisdiction over suspected war criminals,[111] allowing many of them to enjoy impunity for their alleged crimes. The ICC is intended to resolve the problem of in1punity for perpetrators of atrocities,[112] but has led to a different concern, namely, that the ICC may be used by some countries to make trumped-up allegations accusing other states' policymakers, or even implementors of disfavored policies, of engaging in criminal conduct. Probably the most divisive issue at the Rome Conference was the effort to reach a balance between the two extremes - how to bring perpetrators of atrocities to justice while protecting innocent persons from frivolous prosecution and unjust punishment. The conferees finally adopted a somewhat complex system of triggering mechanisms to control how cases were to be referred to the ICC for possible prosecution.

Although the ICC's jurisdiction over the class of suspected criminals is based on the concept of universal jurisdiction for the covered crimes,[113] the ICC may not establish jurisdiction over accused persons unless certain pre-conditions are met. First, unless a case has been referred to the ICC by the U.N. Security Council, the ICC's jurisdiction is complementary to that of national courts: the ICC will try cases only when the state with custody of the accused is unable or unwilling genuinely to prosecute.[114] Where that is determined to be the case, the ICC may take jurisdiction if either the state on whose territory the conduct occurred or the state of nationality of the person accused is a party to the Rome Statute or consents to the jurisdiction of the ICC.

Triggering Mechanisms

There are three avenues through which cases may be referred to the ICC. Either a state party to the Statute, the ICC prosecutor, or the U.N. Security Council[115] may refer cases to the ICC, in accordance with corresponding articles of the Statute. The Security Council may also defer an investigation referred by a state or the prosecutor for a renewable period of 12 months by adopting a resolution under Chapter VII of the U.N. Charter to that effect.[116]

During the negotiations, the United States sought a more powerful role for the Security Council, in which any permanent member would be able to veto a referral. The conferees ultimately rejected this proposal because it was seen to re-introduce political considerations to the prosecutions that are perceived to be responsible for the phenomenon of impunity the ICC is intended to avoid. The Statute as finally adopted allows a single permanent member of the Security Council to veto a *deferral,* allowing the Prosecutor to move forward with a case. With the support of the Permanent Five and four other members of the Security Council, the provision could allow the ICC's exercise of jurisdiction to be forestalled indefinitely.

Referral by a State Party

A state party to the ICC may refer a "situation" to the Prosecutor for investigation where it appears that one or more crimes under the jurisdiction of the ICC have been committed.[117] The referral must be made in writing,[118] and as far as possible, must specify the relevant circumstances and be accompanied by all of the supporting documentation available to the referring state.[119] There is no requirement that the referring state have territorial jurisdiction to prosecute the crime or custody of the alleged perpetrators. If the Prosecutor determines there is sufficient cause to commence an investigation, he or she must notify all states parties and any other state that would normally be able to assert jurisdiction over the crime, possibly on a confidential basis and taking measures to preserve evidence or prevent the absconding of persons.[120]

If a state with conventional jurisdiction notifies the Prosecutor within one month of its intent to investigate the crime, the Prosecutor must defer to that state, but may make an application to the Trial Chamber to commence an investigation on the basis that the state's investigation is not "genuine."[121] The Prosecutor may request the state to provide periodic status reports on the investigation. The decision as to whether a state is "unwilling or unable genuinely" to carry out its investigation is determined by the Pre-Trial Chamber. The state must be informed that the Prosecutor intends to challenge a state's intent or ability to investigate, allowing sufficient time for the state to prepare to present evidence on its behalf. The state may challenge the determination to the Appeals Chamber, and if that challenge is unsuccessful, may later bring a challenge to the admissibility of the case under article 19, providing there are additional facts or a significant change of circumstances.

In the event the Prosecutor decides not to initiate an investigation, the referring state may request a review before the Pre-Trial Chamber,[122] which may request the Prosecutor to reconsider the decision within ninety days following notification.[123] The Pre-Trial Chamber may conduct a review of the Prosecutor's decision on its own motion if the decision is based on the Prosecutor's determination that a prosecution is not in the interest of justice as specified in paragraphs 1(c) or 2(c) of article 53. The decision of the Pre-Trial Chamber in this case is controlling. If new information or evidence becomes available after the Prosecutor has decided not to investigate or if the Pre-Trial Chamber does not authorize an investigation, the Prosecutor may initiate a new investigation.[124]

Initiation by Prosecutor

If the Prosecutor becomes aware of possible crimes within the jurisdiction of the ICC, he or she may commence self-initiated. investigation. There does not appear to be any limitation on how the Prosecutor receives the information or who can submit it. The Prosecutor may request information from states, non-governmental organizations (NGOs), or any other reliable source as deemed appropriate, and must protect the confidentiality of all such information in accordance with the Rome Statute and Rules of Procedure and Evidence.[125] If the Prosecutor concludes that there is a "reasonable basis" for an investigation in a given situation, he or she must first submit a request to the Pre-Trial Chamber for authorization to proceed. The Chamber, in turn, must determine both that there is a "reasonable basis" to proceed with an investigation and that "the case appears to fall within the jurisdiction of the Court." Victims may make presentations to the Pre-Trial Chamber, but there does not appear to be an opportunity for a state with jurisdiction to intercede at this juncture. Once the investigation is authorized, the Prosecutor must notify relevant parties as in the case of a referral by a state party.[126] At that time, a state with jurisdiction over the crime may submit its request for deferral.

If the Prosecutor determines that sufficient basis for an investigation does not exist, he or she must inform those who provided the information,[127] but there is no opportunity for the referring persons or entities to challenge the decision. However, the Pre-Trial Chamber may initiate its own review, giving the Prosecutor a deadline for the submission of observations.[128]

As noted above, the U.N. Security Council may issue a stay preventing the Prosecutor from proceeding in cases submitted by states parties or initiated by the Prosecutor. There does not appear to be a provision in the Rome Statute or Draft RPE stating when, if ever, any organ of the ICC is required to inform the Security Council of an investigation under consideration. Moreover, before the Security Council can act under Chapter VII of the U.N. Charter, as required to defer an investigation under art. 16 of the Rome Statute, the Council must first determine there is "a threat to the peace, breach of the peace or act of aggression. . . ."[129]

Referral by the U.N. Security Council

One of the reasons for initiating an international criminal court was to give the Security Council a permanent forum for war crimes trials, without necessitating the intense effort required to set up an *ad hoc* tribunal. The Security Council may thus, pursuant to its mandate under Chapter VII of the U.N. Charter, refer a case to the Prosecutor for investigation.[130] Presumably, however, the U.N. Security Council is not precluded from initiating a separate *ad hoc* tribunal if for some reason it were to determine that the ICC would be unable to conduct a fair and effective trial, although some predict that the ICC will bring an end to the use of such tribunals.[131]

Once the Prosecutor receives a referral by the U.N. Security Council, he or she determines whether or not an investigation is warranted using the same procedure as in the case of any other type of referral. The Security Council may request that the Pre-Trial Chamber review a decision of the Prosecutor not to initiate an investigation, but may not *require* the Prosecutor to proceed. The most important difference between a referral by the Security Council and the other types of referrals is that the consent of neither the state of nationality of the accused nor the state on whose territory the crime was committed is necessary for the ICC to assert its jurisdiction. The Prosecutor need not inform states with jurisdiction in accordance with art.18, in order to give such states the opportunity to request deferral; however, it appears that those states retain the right to contest the jurisdiction of the ICC based on complementarity.

ICC Jurisdiction over Citizens of Non-Parties

The above-outlined triggering mechanisms for jurisdiction of the ICC make it possible for the ICC to investigate and try citizens of states that have not signed or ratified the Rome Statute. Thus, under certain circumstances the ICC could exercise jurisdiction over a U.S. citizen accused of one or more of the crimes specified in the treaty, even if the United States does not ratify it. If the United States voluntarily consents to the exercise of ICC jurisdiction, or if the state on whose territory an American citizen has allegedly committed the crime consents, the ICC could try a case despite the fact that neither state has ratified the treaty.[132] If an American citizen is accused of committing one of the covered crimes on the territory of a state party, consent is automatic on the part of the territorial state, but either state can supercede the ICC's jurisdiction by undertaking to prosecute the crime in its domestic courts.

Thus, U.S. nationals could be subject to investigation and trial by the ICC if the country in which the alleged crime occurred is either a party to the Rome Statute or consents to the ICC's jurisdiction, and has or is able to gain custody of the alleged U.S. offender. This possibility appears to exist mainly with respect to U.S. military personnel stationed or found in such a country. It also appears to exist with respect to U.S. public officials whose actions are alleged to have caused one of the crimes designated in the Rome Statute, should that official be found in (or extradited to) the country where the crime allegedly occurred.[133] Such exercises of jurisdiction over U.S. nationals could occur pursuant to the initiative of the state where the crime allegedly occurred or of the Prosecutor.[134]

Given the nature of acts covered as crimes that can be prosecuted by the ICC, it is thought to be a rare situation in which an American citizen acting in his or her own capacity could commit such a crime. Americans who are not service members or government officials could, at present, presumably fall under the jurisdiction of the ICC only if they participate in insurgencies abroad or commit any of the covered acts on behalf of a foreign government or entity. If the United States is able to and does assert jurisdiction over the crime and the accused, the ICC could not proceed with prosecution unless it were to find the United States unwilling or unable genuinely to investigate or prosecute the crime. If another country has jurisdiction and decides to surrender a U.S. person accused of a covered crime to the ICC, the United States could appeal the jurisdiction of the ICC.[135]

If the jurisdiction of the ICC eventually is expanded to include terrorism and drug trafficking, there is arguably a greater probability that Americans abroad could be tried by the ICC, as those crimes may not require as a prerequisite a showing that they are part of a greater scheme. However, it has been noted, Americans abroad who are accused of perpetrating a terrorist act or engaging in illicit drug trade are subject to the laws and legal system of the country where the crime took place, without regard to whether the United States consents to such jurisdiction. Some observers have raised the possibility, therefore, that in such cases accused Americans could conceivably enjoy more comprehensive procedural due process rights before the ICC than they would receive in the domestic courts of some foreign states.

Complementarity and Other Challenges to Jurisdiction

According to Article 17 of the Rome Statute, the ICC must find it has no jurisdiction where a state with jurisdiction is investigating or prosecuting the crime, or has investigated the case and genuinely determined that prosecution of the person is unwarranted.[136] The ICC shall determine a case is inadmissible if the accused has already stood trial for the conduct unless it determines the trial was conducted solely for the purpose of shielding the individual from prosecution by the ICC or if it was otherwise conducted in a manner "inconsistent with an intent to bring the person concerned to justice."[137] In order to give the appropriate states the opportunity to take charge of a given situation, the Prosecutor is required to inform all states parties and other interested states when there is a "reasonable basis to commence an investigation" (except in cases referred by the Security Council).[138]

The United States may thus challenge the ICC's jurisdiction over its national in a preliminary proceeding on the basis that it is willing and able to undertake investigation itself. The Statute also provides that a state "from which acceptance of jurisdiction is required under article 12" may challenge the court's jurisdiction.[139] Presumably, the United States could challenge the ICC's jurisdiction over a crime allegedly committed by its national even if no U.S. court has jurisdiction over the crime, by challenging one of the other prerequisites for admissibility of the case. For example, the United States could argue the gravity of the crime of which its national is accused is not sufficiently severe to warrant a trial at the ICC, or that the crime is merely an isolated incident and not part of a larger campaign as required for covered crimes.[140]

Thus, many supporters of the Rome Statute believe that the principle of complementarity, properly applied, is sufficient to insulate U.S. service members and civilians from prosecution at the ICC. After all, they argue, it is virtually inconceivable that the American judicial system will suffer such a massive breakdown as one that would render it "unable to obtain the accused or the necessary evidence and testimony or otherwise unable to carry out its proceedings."[141] Neither is it likely that the United States would be unwilling to investigate alleged atrocities committed by its own troops or officials abroad.[142] Some have suggested that changes in U.S. statutes to broaden the jurisdiction of federal courts to cover all crimes over which the ICC might assert jurisdiction could enhance the implementation of complementarity by precluding a finding by the ICC that the United States is "unable" to prosecute one of its citizens.[143] Opponents of the ICC, however, question whether complementarity will operate as promised, or whether the ICC judges will focus on a perceived deficiency in U.S. trial or court-martial practice to declare that a particular U.S. prosecution or investigation was not conducted in a manner consistent with "the intent to bring the person concerned to justice."[144]

Thus, the primary issue regarding complementarity is the extent to which the ICC will defer to national decisions regarding the handling of purported crimes under the jurisdiction of the ICC. It is unclear, for example, whether the ICC would defer to a decision by a nation to constitute a truth and reconciliation commission, where such a commission could grant amnesty to the perpetrators of genocide in exchange for a full accounting of the events underlying the charge. The granting of amnesty is arguably contrary to the intent to bring criminals to justice, but a nation recovering from the effects of genocide might find it in its interest to form such a commission rather than try to prosecute the alleged perpetrators.[145]

RULES OF PROCEDURE AND EVIDENCE

The Rome Statute contains a comprehensive set of procedural safeguards for the rights of the accused. While some legal experts agree that the Rome Statute contains "the most comprehensive list of due process protections which has so far been promulgated,"[146] some of the ICC's detractors maintain that the procedures nevertheless fall short of U.S. constitutional standards of due process.[147] Some observers caution that the attempt to create a hybrid set of rules, mixing ideas from the common law and civil law traditions, may lead to unpredictable and possibly unjust results.[148]

The Preparatory Commission completed its draft of the Rules of Procedure and Evidence[149] at its Fifth Session in June of 2000. These rules implement and embellish the procedural aspects of the Rome Statute, and are subject to approval by the Assembly of States Parties at its first meeting. A summary comparison of some procedural safeguards in the Rome Statute and those mandated by the U.S. Constitution is set out below.[150]

The Right to a Jury Trial

The Rome Statute does not provide for trial by jury; instead, it follows the civil law tradition of employing a panel of judges to decide questions of both fact and law. This issue does not appear to have been a major point of contention for

U.S. participants during the negotiations of the Rome Statute. This may be true because the Americans considered most at risk, U.S. service members, are subject to court martial under the Uniform Code of Military Justice (UCMJ) and are not entitled to trial by civil jury.[151] American civilians who are accused of crimes overseas are subject to the jurisdiction of the country where the crime took place, and may be tried under that country's laws, which in many cases do not include the right to a trial by jury.

Some opponents of the Rome Treaty argue that it would be unconstitutional for the United States to ratify the Rome Statute because U.S. participation in any court that does not provide for a jury trial in cases where the Constitution requires one would be unlawful.[152] The center position to this argument is that the Constitution does not bar trial by military commission without a Jury under certain circumstances,[153] even the trial of American citizens not members of the armed forces.[154] They also note that the United States has participated in international courts previously, even where American citizens could be tried before them.[155] Finally, the Supreme Court has ruled that persons may be extradited to stand trial in a foreign country despite the lack of jury trial and other procedural safeguards that would be available to that same person if tried in U.S. courts.[156]

The Presumption of Innocence

The Rome Statute provides that "[e]veryone shall be presumed to be innocent until proven guilty before the Court."[157] It also places the burden of proof on the Prosecutor and sets the standard for a conviction to proof beyond a reasonable doubt.[158] The Prosecutor must first have confirmed by the Pre-Trial Chamber that there are sufficient grounds to believe the accused committed the crime as charged.[159] The accused may object to the charges, challenge the evidence against him, or present his own evidence.[160] Once the Pre-Trial Chamber has confirmed the charges, the case will come before a Trial Chamber, which must ensure the accused understands the nature of the charges and then allow the accused to enter a plea of innocence or make an admission of guilt.[161] If the accused has admitted guilt, the Trial Chamber must review the evidence to ensure it is sufficient to support the admission.[162] If the Trial Chamber is not satisfied that the evidence is sufficient, it will proceed with the trial as if the accused entered a plea of innocence.[163] The Trial Chamber is not bound by any plea agreements the Prosecutor may have made with the accused.[164]

In U.S. courts, the accused is entitled to appear in court "without unnecessary physical restraints or other indicia of guilt, such as appearing in prison uniform, that may be prejudicial to the jury."[165] The ICC rules provide that any instruments of restraint "shall be removed when the person appears before a Chamber."[166] The rules do not specify whether military personnel are entitled to appear in uniform before the court.

The Privilege Against Compelled Self-Incrimination

During an investigation, if there is reason to believe a person has committed a crime under the jurisdiction of the ICC, that person has the right "[t]o remain silent, without such silence being a consideration in the determination of guilt or innocence."[167] Any individual questioned during an investigation "[s]hall not be compelled to incriminate himself or herself or to confess guilt; [and s]hall not be subjected to any form of coercion, duress or threat, to torture or to any other form of cruel, inhuman or degrading treatment or punishment;"[168] At the initial stages of an investigation or prosecution, in fact, the Rome Statute may provide broader protection than does the U.S. Constitution the Miranda Rule requires oral notice of rights only when a defendant is interrogated in police custody;[169] the ICC statute requires such a warning whenever the prosecution has grounds to believe that the person being questioned has committed a crime. The defendant also has a right not to testify before the ICC or to refuse to make incriminating statements.[170] A defendant's invocation of the right to remain silent may not be used by the judges in determining the guilt or innocence of the defendant.[171] This safeguard appears to be analogous to the Fifth Amendment to the Constitution.

Witnesses may refuse to give testimony that might incriminate them. The ICC has the authority to give assurances to the witness that he or she will not be prosecuted or detained by the ICC for conduct prior to departure from the requested state or for incriminating testimony.[172] The ICC may also allow in camera testimony by the witness, giving assurances that the content of the testimony will not be disclosed to the public or any state.[173] Unless the ICC grants such assurances, the witness may not be compelled to answer.[174] Presumably, the right to avoid self-incrimination would extend beyond the crimes triable by the ICC to evidence which could credibly lead to prosecution by a state. It is not clear whether the ICC would respect the immunity of witnesses or accused persons granted by states, or whether it would exclude compelled testimony taken by officials of a state.

The Right to Confront Witnesses

The Rome Statute provides that "the accused shall be entitled . . . to examine, or to have examined . . . the witnesses against him or her . . . [and] to obtain the attendance and examination of witnesses on his or her behalf..."[175] There is an exception, however, in cases where the alleged crime involves sexual violence or violence against children.[176] The ICC may invoke procedures to protect the identities of victims if such protection is deemed necessary.[177] Such procedures include live testimony by means of audio-visual broadcast "provided that such technology permits the witness to be examined by the Prosecutor, the defense, and by the Chamber itself, at the time that the witness so testifies," and "is conducive to the giving of truthful and open testimony and to the safety, physical and psychological well-being, dignity and privacy of the witness.[178]

U.S. law prohibits (with exceptions) the use of out-of-court statements to prove the truth of the matter stated, otherwise known as "hearsay" evidence.[179] The Rome Statute and Draft RPE do not explicitly provide for a similar rule. If the practice of the International Criminal Tribunal for the Former Yugoslavia (ICFY) is followed, hearsay evidence will likely be admissible on a more frequent basis than in U.S. courts. In civil law courts, hearsay evidence is not considered to be unduly prejudicial in most cases because the judges, unlike lay jurors, are presumed to be capable of accurately assessing the credibility of hearsay evidence and discounting any prejudicial content.

The United States Supreme Court has recognized the need for special measures for the protection of witnesses in some criminal trials, notwithstanding the defendant's right to face his accusers.[180] Measures such as one-way closed circuit television system may be employed to protect a child witness who might suffer emotional trauma at the sight of the accused, as long as sufficient safeguards were in place to preserve rigorous adversarial testing of the testimony.[181] Similar to the procedure approved by the Supreme Court, the Rome Statute provisions for protective measures must be ordered by the ICC taking into consideration all the relevant circumstances,[182] and such measures "shall not be prejudicial to or inconsistent with the rights of the accused and a fair and impartial trial."[183]

The Protection Against Double Jeopardy

The Statute bars the ICC from trying any person who has been tried and convicted or acquitted by another court, unless that trial was for the purpose of "shielding the person concerned from criminal responsibility" or was otherwise "inconsistent with an intent to bring the person concerned to justice."[184] The *ne bis in idem* rule in the Rome Statute is in some ways more protective of the accused than the United States Constitution, which allows a person to be tried by more than one sovereign (federal or state court) or in some cases, for a separate crime arising out of the same conduct.[185] In contrast, the Rome Statute specifies the ICC may not try a person who has been tried by any other court for the same conduct, unless it finds the : trial or investigation to be improper for one of the enumerated reasons. Thus, the danger of the ICC trying a person who has already been tried by a national court will ultimately depend on the ICC's deference to national judicial decisions.[186]

The Rome Statute further provides that "no person shall be tried by another court for a crime" for which the ICC has already convicted or acquitted the person.[187] Non-parties would not be bound by this rule, however, so a person tried by the ICC could conceivably be tried again by the court of a non-party state, or possibly even by a party to the Statute that seeks to punish the same conduct under another criminal charge.

Another issue that raises possible double jeopardy implications is the prosecutorial appeal of an acquittal.[188] Under U.S. law, prosecutors may appeal only on questions of law, but may not appeal a final acquittal.[189] The Rome Statute allows the Prosecutor to appeal any decision based on procedural error, error of fact, or error of law. The defendant may also appeal on these grounds, as well as "any other ground that affects the fairness or reliability of the proceedings."[190]

The Freedom from Unreasonable Searches and Seizures

Although the Rome Statute does not contain an express reference to the right to be free from unreasonable searches and seizures, it does provide for an exclusionary rule to prevent evidence tainted by a violation of "internationally recognized human rights."[191] The ICC will not apply national law to determine the admissibility of evidence unless it is consistent with the Rome Statute as well as treaties, principles, and rules of international law.[192] Consequently, accused persons are protected from unreasonable searches and seizures to the extent that international law forbids them. The right to privacy against such intrusion is protected under a number of international documents and treaties, including the Universal Declaration of Human Rights (UDHR)[193] and the International

Covenant on Civil and Political Rights (ICCPR),[194] both of which have been ratified by a majority of nations participating at the Rome Conference.[195]

Such a standard may turn out to be higher than that applied by U.S. courts in certain cases, inasmuch as U.S. courts apply a lower standard in the event that evidence was gathered outside the territorial jurisdiction of the United States.[196] However, the ICC need not necessarily consider, for example, whether a search warrant should have been necessary. Because evidence is likely to be collected either by or with the cooperation of national law enforcement authorities, investigators will probably find it necessary to rely on national laws rather than try to discern international norms to guide the conduct of the investigation. It may therefore emerge from the ICC's practice that national laws carry more weight than the Rome Statute would suggest. At any rate, any comparison between the ICC and U.S. courts' practice with regard to tainted evidence must await the ICC's development of relevant practice. In particular, the extent to which the exclusionary rule of the ICC will apply to evidence *derived* from unlawfully seized evidence remains to be seen.

The Right to Be Present at Trial

The Rome Statute provides that "[t]he accused shall be present during the trial."[197] The Trial Chamber may order the accused removed from the courtroom in exceptional circumstances when the accused causes continuous disruption, but only for such duration as is necessary, and may make provision for the accused to observe the trial and direct counsel from outside the courtroom through applicable communications technology.[198]

In U.S. jurisprudence, the Confrontation Clause of Amendment VI guarantees the accused's right to be present in the courtroom at every stage of his trial.[199] However, as long as the defendant is present at the beginning of the trial, the trial will not be rendered invalid if the defendant voluntarily absents himself during later stages of the trial.[200] The Rome Statute does not address the voluntary absence of the accused once the trial begins.

The Right to Effective Assistance of Counsel

Article 67 of the Rome Statute provides that "the accused shall be entitled . . . to have legal assistance assigned by the Court where the interests of justice so require, and without payment if the accused lacks sufficient means to pay for it."[201]

Defense counsel must also be well-qualified[202] according to criteria to be established.[203] The Registrar has a duty to provide adequate administrative support to the defense.[204] The Statute also guarantees that "the accused shall be entitled . . . to communicate freely with counsel of accused's choosing."[205] Similar to the attorney-client privilege practiced in the U.S. judicial system.[206] Draft RPE 73 provides that such communications are privileged and need not be disclosed at trial.

The Right to a Speedy and Public Trial

The U.S. Constitution guarantees the right to a speedy and public trial.[207] Similarly, the Rome Statute provides that the accused is entitled to be tried "without undue delay" by means of a public hearing.[208]

Speedy Trial

In U.S. federal courts, criminal trials generally must commence within seventy days after an indictment or original appearance before the court.[209] In courts-martial, the time limit is 120 days from the preferral of charges or the imposition of restraint, whichever date is earliest.[210] Statutes of limitations for crimes also guard against undue delay between the government's discovery of evidence and its prosecution of an accused person. A denial of the right to a speedy trial results in a dismissal of the indictment.[211] However, if the accused is found to have waived the right, or the circumstances and justice otherwise require it, a delay may not be fatal to the prosecution.[212] In determining whether the right has been denied, a court may consider such factors as the length of the delay, the reason for the delay, whether the defendant asserted his right to a speedy trial, and the prejudice to the defendant caused by the delay.[213]

The Rome Statute does not define "undue delay." The Draft RPE instruct the Trial Chamber to impose "strict time limits" for orders relating to discovery.[214] Draft RPE 101 provides:

In making any order setting time limits regarding the conduct of any proceedings, the Court shall have regard to the need to facilitate fair and expeditious proceedings, bearing in mind in particular the rights of the defense and the victims.

The Rome Statute does not provide a statute of limitation for any of the crimes under its jurisdiction.[215] Under U.S. law, there is no statute of limitation for the crime of genocide[216] or for any crime for which the death penalty may be imposed,[217] which includes any war crime that causes the death of its victim,[218] or any terrorism-related offense that involves the risk of death or serious injury.[219] For non-capital crimes, however, the statute of limitation is generally five years.[220]

Public Trial

In U.S. courts, closure of the courtroom during trial proceedings is justified only if 1) the proponent of closure advances an overriding interest likely to be prejudiced; 2) the closure is no broader than necessary; 3) the trial court considers reasonable alternatives to closure; and 4) the trial court makes findings adequate to support closure.[221] The right to a public trial in courts-martial is also guaranteed, but not absolute.[222] A defendant may request a closed trial, but must meet the same stringent standards applied to a request by the prosecution. Additionally, the press and public have a First Amendment right to have access to trials,[223] which must sometimes be considered in addition to the other factors.

The Rome Statute provides for public hearing unless "special circumstances require that certain proceedings be in closed session for the purposes set forth in article 68 [to protect witnesses or victims], or to protect confidential or sensitive information to be given in evidence."[224] The Trial Chamber must first give all parties notice and the opportunity to respond to any proposed special protective procedures.[225] Possible protective measures include the use of a pseudonym or technological disguise measures for witnesses, gag orders for certain information as well as its removal from the public record, or the closure of part of the hearing.[226] Additionally, any state may make an application to the ICC for necessary measures to protect its agents or sensitive national security information.[227]

Right to Appeal

Either the defendant or the prosecutor can appeal a decision of the Trial Chamber to the Appeals Chamber based on "procedural error, error of fact or law, or disproportion between the crime and the sentence." The accused or his heirs may bring an appeal at any time based on new evidence or information that the conviction is based on false evidence, or that any of the judges or prosecutors committed any misdeeds.[228]

The ICC's opponents criticize the appeal process as inadequate because it does not provide for review outside the ICC.[229] As discussed above, the conferees sought to implement checks and balances as well as create a separation between the Appeals Division and the other trial divisions. It might also be noted that prior to 1993, international criminal courts did not include an appellate body,[230] nor did national courts review the decisions of such tribunals.[231] Practice in the International Criminal Tribunal for Yugoslavia (ICTY) and the International Criminal Tribunal for Rwanda (ICTR) suggests that an appellate body within an international court may not always necessarily affirm the decisions of trial chambers.[232]

Freedom from Indefinite or Arbitrary Detention

The Fourth Amendment to the U.S. Constitution protects persons from unreasonable seizures, including the arrest of a person without probable cause,[233] and sometimes, without a warrant. A person unlawfully arrested is not automatically released from custody,[234] however, although evidence derived through the unlawful arrest may be excludable from evidence.[235] The Fifth Amendment protects individuals from deprivation of liberty without due process of law. The Rome Statute contains corresponding safeguards to prevent the arbitrary arrest and detention of persons,[236] and includes provisions for interim release of the accused prior to trial.[237] Because the ICC has no law enforcement arm, relying instead largely on states to provide for the arrest and detention of accused persons using national police resources, however, the procedures may vary depending on the state of custody.

The Prosecutor must seek an arrest warrant or a summons from the Pre-Trial Chamber when necessary to ensure an accused's appearance at trial.[238] The application must identify the person and the crime of which the person is accused, including a concise statement of facts supporting the allegation and a summary of evidence. On the basis of, the warrant, the ICC may request the provisional arrest or arrest and surrender under part 9 of the Rome Statute. The ICC is required to establish procedures for ensuring it is notified once a person is detained by a custodial state on the request of the ICC, and must provide a copy of the warrant to the accused in a language he or she understands.[239]

The Pre-Trial Chamber is to receive notification whenever a detainee has requested interim release in accordance with the laws of the custodial state, and makes recommendations to the national court as to the suitability of release.[240] The custodial state is not permitted to consider whether the warrant was properly issued under the Rome Statute,[241] but the accused may challenge the warrant before the Pre-Trial Chamber.[242] If the accused is in the custody of the ICC, the accused may apply for interim release pending trial, which the Pre-Trial Chan1ber may grant with or without conditions.[243] If the person is detained for an unreasonable period prior to trial due to inexcusable delay by the Prosecutor, the ICC may release the person, with or without conditions.[244] A person wrongfully arrested, detained, or convicted may be awarded compensation by the ICC.[245]

Once a person is convicted, the ICC will select from states willing to serve as "state of enforcement" to incarcerate the convicted person subject to any ICC conditions. The prisoner may not be tried, punished, or extradited to a third state for conduct engaged in prior to the person's incarceration without the approval of the ICC.[246] In designating a state of enforcement, the ICC must consider:

(a) The principle that states parties should share the responsibility for enforcing sentences of imprisonment, in accordance with principles of equitable distribution, as provided in the Rules of Procedure and Evidence;

(b) The application of widely accepted international treaty standards governing the treatment of prisoners;

(c) The views of the sentenced person;

(d) The nationality of the sentenced person; and

(e) Such other factors regarding the circumstances of the crime or the person sentenced, or the effective enforcement of the sentence, as may be appropriate in designating the state of enforcement.[247]

Additionally, the ICC will monitor the treatment of the prisoner, and the prisoner may petition to be moved to another state of enforcement at any time.[248]

IMPLICATIONS FOR THE UNITED STATES AS NON-MEMBER

The U.S. initially used the proceedings of the Preparatory Commission in part as a means of trying to rectify what it saw as the faults of the Rome Statute, and it participated as an equal during the initial conferences.[249] However, the current Administration has reduced the level of the U.S. participation,[250] and in any event, the Preparatory Commission will cease to exist after the first meeting of the Assembly of States Parties; U.S. eligibility to participate on an equal basis with other states in setting some of the ground rules for the ICC will then have ended. The Assembly of States Parties will take over as the governing body to oversee the implementation and possible amendment of the Rome Statute. Review Conferences are an alternative forum for considering amendments to the Statute; an initial Review Conference will be convened seven years after the Statute enters into effect, now expected to be July 2002. Thereafter, Review Conferences may be convened from time to time by the U.N. Secretary-General upon request by a majority of the states parties.[251] As a non-party, the United States will have no vote in either body. However, it will remain eligible to participate in both the Assembly and in Review Conferences as an observer.[252]

Observer Role

The role of observers ultimately will be defined by the rules of procedure adopted for the two bodies.[253] If the current finalized draft rules are adopted, observers will be entitled to participate in the deliberations of the Assembly and any subsidiary bodies that might be established. Observer states will receive notifications of all meetings and records of Assembly proceedings on the same basis as states parties. They will not, however, be permitted to suggest items for the agenda or to make motions during debate, such as points of order or motions for adjournment. Thus, the United States may be able to participate substantially in Assembly debates as well as proffer and respond to proposals, even if it does not become a party to the Statute. The United States may also use its influence at the United Nations as a way to be heard by the Assembly of States Parties.[254]

As noted, the United States will not be able to vote in these bodies if it does not ratify the Rome Statute. It could not nominate U.S. nationals to serve as judges or cast a vote in elections for judges or the Prosecutor (or for their removal). It could not vote on the ICC's budget. It could not vote on the definition of the crime of aggression or its inclusion within the jurisdiction of the ICC, when the matter is considered at first Review Conference, or on any other amendment to the Rome Statute.

The United States, as a non-party, will have no right itself to refer situations to the Prosecutor for investigation; as a Permanent Member of the Security Council, however, it could participate as part of a Security Council referral.[255] Similarly, it could still participate in Security Council requests to the Prosecutor to defer an investigation or prosecution[256] and to the Pre-Trial Chamber to review a decision of the Prosecutor not to investigate or prosecute.[257] As a non-party to the treaty, the United States could, but would not be obligated to, cooperate with the ICC in its investigation and prosecution of crimes within its jurisdiction;[258] and under the Statute, it could, but would not be obligated to, arrest a person named in a request for provisional arrest or for arrest and surrender from the ICC.[259] The U.S. would also retain the right not to provide information or documents the disclosure of which would prejudice its national security interests[260] and to refuse to consent to the disclosure by a state party of information or documents provided to that state in confidence.[261] Finally, as a non-party, the U.S. would not be under any obligation to contribute to the budget for the ICC, except, perhaps indirectly, to the extent that the U.N. General Assembly contributes to its support.[262]

Political Implications

Perspectives differ on the impact of the ICC on U.S. interests, once it begins operation. Some see the ICC as a fundamental threat to the u.s. armed forces, its political leaders, and U.S. defense and foreign policy.[263] Others see it as a valuable foreign policy tool for defining and deterring crimes against humanity, a step forward in the decades-long U.S. effort to end impunity for egregious mass crimes. Debate over the ICC has brought out a tension between enhancing the international legal justice system and encroaching on what some countries perceive as their legitimate use of force. The review by the International Criminal Tribunal for the Former Yugoslavia (ICFY) of allegations that NATO bombing in Kosovo might be deemed a war crime is illustrative of this tension. Many opponents of the ICC and members of the U.S. military were outraged that the issue was even considered. They questioned the legitimacy of the tribunal's actions, and their anger was not assuaged by the Tribunal's ultimate decision that there was "no basis for opening an investigation into any of those allegations or into other incidents relating to NATO bombing."[264] While opponents of the ICC interpret this event as an indication that the ICC is likely to pursue spurious and politically motivated cases against U.S. citizens, proponents of the ICC see it as illustrating that similar unfounded allegations would be dismissed by the ICC Prosecutor.

The United States has often been a leader in the struggle against impunity and the quest for peace, justice and human rights. The United States led the world community in calling for establishment of the ad hoc tribunals for the former Yugoslavia and Rwanda. Supporters of the ICC argue that it could be the ultimate symbol of enforcement of basic human rights norms. Such countries, which include a number of U.S. allies, might view the true test of the U.S. commitment to international and universal concepts of justice and human rights to be its willingness to be bound by the rules established for others. From this perspective, despite the Administration's asserted intent to continue U.S. leadership in supporting human rights through means other than the ICC,[265] the U.S. refusal to ratify the Rome Statute could undermine the status of, and others' regard for, the United States as a proponent of human rights.

Others, however argue that despots like Cambodia's Pol Pot or Iraq's Saddam Hussein have not weighed possible future legal ramifications before committing massive crimes.[266] In their view, establishment of the ICC might have the effect of hardening the resolve of ruthless tyrants who may feel they have nothing to gain by giving up their power to more democratic or less ruthless regimes - as General Pinochet did in Chile or Duvalier in Haiti. The critical element from this perspective is simply the treaty's entry into force, not whether the U.S. ratifies it, other than perhaps to provide support to an argument challenging the legitimacy of the ICC.

U.S. allies, such as France and Canada, which also deploy forces abroad in peacekeeping and other interventions, initially shared U.S. concerns about the ICC' s ability to judge the actions of their nationals particularly with regard to use of force. During negotiations, these countries concluded that the ICC's larger value outweighed any potential risk posed to their nationals or foreign policy. While some Americans fear the ICC could be used for political purposes, many U.S. allies see the ICC as more limited. In their view, the ICC would intervene to prosecute crimes of genocide, crimes against humanity, and war crimes only when a country fails to try its own citizens for committing such acts. Some countries are adopting war crimes provisions as part of their own domestic laws with the thought that the ICC would never be called on to intervene. For example, France amended its constitution before ratifying the Rome Statute.[267]

For the U.S. government, the situation appears to be more complicated. With several hundred thousand persons stationed abroad, often involved in undertakings that might be subject to allegations of war crimes, the United States is particularly cautious. U.S. military leaders are especially concerned that countries that do not ratify the ICC treaty could consent to the ICC's jurisdiction over foreign peacekeeping troops for crimes committed on their territory, while declining to allow the ICC to try the persons responsible for whatever atrocities brought peacekeepers there in the first place.[268] Concern about U.S. citizens being tried by the ICC stem from an underlying fear that a politicized court could be used by hostile states as a vehicle for challenging u.s. foreign policy. Given that the ICC could exercise, jurisdiction over U.S. citizens in some situations even if the U.S. does not ratify the treaty, these concerns seem likely to persist even if the U.S. remains a non-party.

CONGRESSIONAL ACTION

Congress has passed several riders effectively precluding the use of funds to support the ICC.[269] The fundamental issue for Congress is whether to pass legislation to actively oppose the ICC, or whether to adopt a more benign approach aimed at encouraging the ICC to develop in a manner conducive to U.S. policy aims. There are currently two bills in Congress adopting the first approach, and one taking the second tack. The House of Representative added a rider to the Bob Stump National Defense Authorization Act for Fiscal Year 2003, H.R. 4546, expressing the sense of the Congress that "none of the funds appropriated pursuant to authorizations of appropriations in this Act should be used for any assistance to, or to cooperate with or to provide any support for, the International Criminal Court."[270] Additionally, the Administration may ask Congress to pass legislation to close jurisdictional gaps in U.S. criminal law in order to ensure U.S. territory does not become a safe haven for those accused of genocide, war crimes, and crimes against humanity.[271]

American Service Members' Protection Act of 2001

The American Service Members' Protection Act (ASPA) was originally introduced in the 106th Congress as S. 2726. The proposed legislation is intended to shield members of the United States Armed Forces and other covered persons from the jurisdiction of the ICC. The Senate Committee on Foreign Relations held hearings[272] the same day the bill was introduced but did not report it. The ASPA was reintroduced in the 107th Congress as S. 857 on May 9, 2001. An amended version was introduced as S. 1610 on November 1, 2001.

Two versions of the ASPA have been passed by the House of Representatives. The first is contained in the Foreign Relations Authorization Act, Fiscal Years 2002 and 2003, H.R.1646, Title VI, subtitle B. The Senate amended version of H.R. 1646 does not include the ASPA. H.R. 1646 is in conference at the time of this writing. The second version was passed as Title II of the supplemental appropriations bill for the fiscal year ending September 30, 2002, H.R. 4775.

The Senate also passed a version of the ASPA, as part of the Departments of Commerce, Justice, and State, the Judiciary, and Related Agencies Appropriations Act, 2002, HR 3338, but it was replaced in the enacted law with language prohibiting spending to support the ICC.[273] Title II of H.R. 4775 is substantially similar to S. 857 (H.R. 1794), and would repeal the provision passed as part of H.R. 3338. Title VI, subtitle B of H.R. 1646 is summarized below, followed by a description of the additional language contained in Title II of H.R. 4775.

The ASPA would prohibit cooperation with the ICC on the part of any agency or entity of the federal government, or any state or local government. (Sec. 634) Covered entities are prohibited from responding to a request for cooperation by the ICC or providing specific assistance, including arrest, extradition, seizure of property, asset forfeiture, service of warrants, searches, taking of evidence, and similar matters. It prohibits agents of the ICC from conducting any investigative activity on U.S. soil related to matters of the ICC. Sec. 634(d) states that the United States "shall exercise its rights to limit the use of assistance provided under all treaties and executive agreements for mutual legal assistance in criminal matters . . . to prevent . . . use by the [ICC of such assistance]." It does not ban the communication to the ICC of U.S. policy or assistance to defendants. Sec. 636 requires the President to put "appropriate procedures" in place to prevent the direct or indirect transfer of certain classified national security information to the ICC.

The ASPA would further restrict U.S. participation in U.N. peacekeeping operations to missions where the President certifies U.S. troops may participate without risk of prosecution by the ICC because the Security Council permanently exempted U.S. personnel for prosecution for activity conducted as participants, or because each other country participating in the mission is either not a party to the ICC and does not consent to its jurisdiction, or has entered into an agreement "in accordance with article 98" of the Rome Statute.[274] It also prohibits military assistance to any non-NATO country that is member of the ICC, unless the President waives the restriction (Sec. 637).

Sec. 638 authorizes the President to use "all means necessary and appropriate" to bring about the release of covered United States and allied persons,[275] upon the request of the detainee's government, who are being detained or imprisoned by or on behalf of the ICC. The Act does not provide a definition of "necessary and appropriate means" to bring about the release of covered persons, other than to exclude bribes and the provision of other such incentives. The language could arguably be interpreted to authorize the use of armed force to conduct rescue operations to free some prisoners charged with war crimes, genocide, or crimes against humanity.

The President may waive the restrictions on participation in peacekeeping operations and providing military assistance for a renewable period of one year after notifying appropriate congressional committees of his intent to do so and reporting that the ICC has entered into a binding agreement that prohibits it from exercising jurisdiction over covered u.s. and allied persons (from certain countries for so long as those countries have not ratified the treaty). (Sec. 633) The President may also waive some requirements with respect to a specific "named individual," if there is reason to believe the named individual is guilty of the charge, it is in the national interest of the United States for the ICC to prosecute the person, and that during the investigation, no covered U.S. or allied person will be arrested, detained, prosecuted, or imprisoned by or on behalf of the ICC with regard actions taken in their official capacities.

H.R. 4775. The version of the ASPA included in H.R. 4775 (which is substantially similar to the Senate amended version of HR 3338) contains an additional exception at section 2011, stating that the restrictions on cooperation with the ICC (sec. 2004 of H.R. 4775) and protecting classified information (sec. 2006) do not apply to "any action or actions with respect to a specific matter taken or directed by the President on a case-by-case basis in the exercise of the President's authority as Commander in Chief of the Armed Forces of the United States under article II, section 2 of the United States Constitution or in the exercise of the executive power under article II, section 1 of the United States Constitution."276 The section would require the President to notify Congress within 15 days of the action, unless such notification would jeopardize national security. It further clarifies that "nothing in [the] section shall be construed as a grant of statutory authority to the President to take any action." Sec. 2012 prohibits delegation of the authorities vested in the President by secs. 2003 (waiver provision) and 2011(a) (constitutional exception).

Inasmuch as sections 2004 and 2006 are already subject to presidential waiver under section 2003(c) in the case of the investigation or prosecution of a "named individual," it appears that this section is drafted to avoid possible conflicts of the separation of powers between the President and Congress. In the event that the President takes the position that the prohibitions of sections 2004 and 2006 infringe upon his constitutional authority in certain cases, he might assert that Congress has no power even to require a waiver under section 2003. Section 2011 appears to ensure notification of Congress, at least at some point after the action has been taken, regardless of whether the President believes that sections 2004 and 2006 impinge his constitutional authority.

The effect of sec. 2011 is not entirely clear, depending as it does on the interpretation of the President's executive powers under article II, section 1 of the Constitution and his authority as Commander in Chief of the Armed Forces. Interpreted broadly, the constitutional executive power includes the power to execute the law, meaning the execution of *any* law, whether statutory or constitutional, or even international law. Such an interpretation would seem to render the waiver provision of sec. 2003(c) superfluous. Interpreted narrowly, the executive authorities cited above could refer to those powers which the President does not share with Congress. Under a narrow interpretation, Congress would be deemed to be without authority to regulate such actions in any event, in which case it would appear to make little sense to restrict its application to sections 2004 and 2006. The language could be construed by a court to imply a waiver authority apart from the restrictions outlined in section 2003.

The American Service Member and Citizen Protection Act of 2002

The American Service Member and Citizen Protection Act of 2002, H.R. 4169, introduced April 11, 2002, issues findings that under the U.S. Constitution and international law, the President's signature on a treaty without ratification by the Senate is not binding on the United States, and that therefore the ICC Statute has no validity with respect to U.S. The bill proclaims the Rome Statute to be "ultra vires" (sec. 2(9)) and in violation of international law, the American Declaration of Independence, and the Constitution (sec. 2(12)). It also urges the President to rescind the U.S. signature and take steps (sec. 3) to prevent the establishment of the ICC. Sec. 4 prohibits the expenditure of funds for use in any manner for the "establishment or operation of the [ICC]" (with a penalty of 5 years or $50,000 for violations, sec. 6). Sec. 5 provides that actions against U .S; soldiers shall be considered to be an act of aggression, and actions against other U.S. persons shall be considered "to be an offense against the law of nations."

The American Citizens' Protection and
War Criminal Prosecution Act of 2001

This bill, S.1296 (H.R. 2699), seeks a more conciliatory approach to the ICC, providing that the President should certify that the ICC "has established a demonstrated record of fair and impartial prosecution of genocide, war crimes, and crimes against humanity" before the Rome Statute is submitted to the Senate for its advice and consent. (Sec. 10). Sec. 4 provides a sense of the Congress that the United States should "maintain a policy of fully supporting the due process rights of all United States citizens before foreign tribunals, including the [ICC]". It recommends the U.S. government participate as an observer in the Assembly of States Parties in order to ". . .a protect and further U.S. interests. Sec. 8 requires the President to ensure appropriate procedures are in place to protect national security information.

Sec. 5 prohibits the United States from taking any action to extradite U.S. citizens and service members to the ICC if the accused is investigated or prosecuted in a U.S. court, and urges the United States to exercise its right to assert jurisdiction over such persons (to invoke complementarity), unless the President determines it is not in the national interest. If a U.S. citizen is prosecuted by the ICC, the President "shall use appropriate diplomatic and legal resources to ensure that such person receives due process . . ." and provide whatever exculpatory evidence may be available to assist the accused. Sec. 7 authorizes support to the ICC on a case-by-case basis if such support would serve important U.S. interests, particularly if the victims of the crimes alleged are citizens of the United States or friendly countries.

The bill contains a number of reporting requirements for assessments of the operation of the ICC and its effects on U.S. interests. Sec. 6 outlines reporting procedures, requiring the President to compare due process protections afforded to persons before the ICC to those afforded U.S. service members under status of forces agreements, and to bilateral or multilateral extradition treaties. Sec. 5 requires the Administration to conduct a study to determine what statutory amendments may be necessary to close jurisdictional gaps in the criminal code or Uniform Code of Military Justice. Sec. 9 requires a report on command arrangements that could place U.S. service members at risk of prosecution by the ICC and measures taken to mitigate the risks.

REFERENCES

[1]   U.N. Doc. NCONF.183/9 (1988)("Rome Statute").

[2]   These include genocide, crimes against humanity, war crimes, and potentially the crime of aggression, if the Assembly of States Parties is able to reach an agreement defining it. Rome Statute art. 5(1). *See infra* text accompanying note 98.

[3] *See* Barbara Crossette, *World Criminal Court is Ratified - Praised by UN., Opposed by U.S.,* N.Y. TIMES Apr. 12, 2002, *available at* 2002 WL-NYT 0210200003. For the current status of signatures, ratifications and reservations, visit http://untreaty.un.orgi ENGLISH/bible/ english internet bible/partI/chapterXVIII/treaty 10.asp.

[4] *See* Jonathon Wright, *U.S. Renounces Obligations to International Court,* 'REUTERS, May 6, 2002. Although some in the media have described the act as an "unsigning" of the treaty, it may be more accurately described as a notification of intent not to ratify. The letter from Under Secretary of State for Arms Control and International Security John R. Bolton to the U.N. Secretary General stated: This is to inform you, in connection with the Rome Statute of the International Criminal Court adopted on July 17, 1998, that the United States does not intend to become a party to the treaty. Accordingly, the United States has no legal obligations arising from its signature on December 31, 2000. The United States requests that its intention not to become a party, as expressed in this letter, be reflected in the depositary's status lists relating to this treaty. *Reprinted at* http://www.state.gov/r/pa/prs/ps/2002/9968.htm.

[5] *See Give it a Welcome - The Coming World Criminal Court,* ECONOMIST (London), Apr. 13, 2002, available at 2002 WL 7245784; James Bone, War Crimes Court Pits United States Against the World, TIMES OF LONDON, Apr. 11, 2002, available at 2002 WL 4198476; Stuart Taylor Jr., Be Wary of the War Crimes Court, but Not Too Wary, NAT'L J., Apr. 6,2002, available at 2002 WL7094917.

[6] *See* Marc Grossman, Under Secretary for Political Mairs, Remarks to the Center for Strategic and International Studies, Washington, D.C., (May 6, 2002) (prepared remarks available at http://www.state.gov/p/9949pf.htm). Secretary Grossman promised that: Notwithstanding our disagreements with the Rome Treaty, the United States respects the decision of those nations who have chosen to join the ICC; but they in turn must respect our decision not to join the ICC or place our citizens under the jurisdiction of the court. So, despite this difference, we must work together to promote real justice after July 1, when the Rome Statute enters into force. The existence of a functioning ICC will not cause the United States to retreat from its leadership role in the promotion of international justice and the rule of law.

[7] *See* Colum Lynch, *U.S. Seeb Court Immunity for E. Timor Peacekeepers,* WASH. POST May 16,2002 at A22, *available at* 2002 WL 20709611 (reporting there are currently no U.S. troops serving in U.N. missions); Edith M. Lederer, *U.S. Makes Int'l Court Demands,* AP May 20, 2002,

available at 2002 WL 21234979 (reporting that France, Britain, Ireland, Norway, and Colombia oppose the U.S. request).

[8]   *See* Ruth Wedgwood, Harold K. Jacobson and Monroe Leigh, *The United States and the Statute of Rome,* 95 AM. J. INT'L L. 124 (2001) (commenting that the United States has "repeatedly and publicly declared its support in principle" for an international criminal court). Congress expressed its support for such a court, providing the rights of U.S. citizens were recognized. *See, e.g.,* Foreign Operations Appropriations Act § 599E, P.L. 101-513, 104 Stat. 2066-2067 (1990)(expressing the sense of the Congress that "the United States should explore the need for the establishment of an International Criminal Court" and that "the establishment of such a court or courts for the more effective prosecution of international criminals should not derogate from established standards of due process, the rights of the accused to a fair trial and the sovereignty of individual nations"); Anti-Drug Abuse Act of 1988 § 4108, P.L. 100-690, 102 Stat. 4181, 4266 (1988)(encouraging the President to initiate discussions with foreign governments about the possibility of creating an international court to try persons accused of having engaged in international drug trafficking or having committed international crimes, providing constitutional guarantees of U.S. citizens are recognized); P.L. 99-399, Sec. 1201 (1986)

[9]   See U.N. International Criminal Court: Hearings before the Subcomm. on International Operations of the Senate Foreign Relations Committee 105tb Congo (1998) (testimony of David J. Scheffer, Ambassador-at-Large for War Crimes Issues).

[10]   *See* Wedgwood, *et al., supra* note 8, at 124 (noting that the final vote for the Statute was 120 in favor to seven against).

[11]   Statement on the Rome Treaty on the International Criminal Court, Dec. 31, 2000, 37(1) Weekly Compilation of Presidential Documents 4 (2001).

[12]   Because the United States signed the Rome Statute, it had been obligated under international law to refrain from conducting activity in contravention of the object and purpose of the treaty. *See* Vienna Convention on the Law of Treaties, *opened for signature* May 23,1969, art. 1§, 1155 U.N.T.S. 335. However, this obligation ends once a signatory state has indicated an intent *not* to ratify the treaty. *Id.* Some press reports initially indicated the Administration was also planning to renounce the Vienna Convention. *See* Neil A. Lewis, *U.S. to 'Unsign' Treaty, Disavow World Tribunal,* SAN DIEGO UNION & TRIB., May 5,2002 at AI. The report was apparently based on a misunderstanding of the Administration's statement explaining

the intent behind its action, which was reportedly to avoid any obligations on the part of the United States that may have been incurred through its signature of the Rome Statute, in accordance with article 18 of the Vienna Convention.

[13] *See* Grossman, *supra* note 6.

[14] *See* David J. Scheffer, *Staying the Course with the International Criminal Court,* 35 CORNELL INT'L L.J. 47 (2000) (arguing the United States could most effectively influence the shape of the ICC through cooperating with it rather than impeding it).

[15] For a general background and discussion of the ICC, see The Rome Statute of the International Criminal Court: Selected Legal and Constitutional Issues, CRS Report RL30091, Feb. 22, 1999; The International Criminal Court Treaty: Description, Policy Issues, and Congressional Concerns, CRS Report RL30020, Jan. 5, 1999.

[16] GA Res. 49/53, U.N. GAOR, 49th Sess., U.N. Doc. NRES/49/53 (1994).

[17] GA Res. 50/46, U.N. GAOR, 50th Sess., U.N. Doc. A/RES/50/46 (1995).

[18] *See* United Nations, "The Draft Statute of the International Criminal Court: Background Information," *available at* http://www.un.org/icc/statute.htm.

[19] Rome Statute arts. 12-14.

[20] *See* Johan D. van der Vyver, *Personal and Territorial Jurisdiction of the International Criminal Court,* 14 EMORY INT'L L. REV. 1, 32 (2000).

[21] *See* Wedgwood, *et ai, supra* note 8, at 126 (commenting that the U.S. proposal would "exempt not only U.S. nationals, but also the nationals of rogue states, which are most likely to produce or to harbor war criminals in the future and which are the least likely to consent to having their nationals tried by the ICC").

[22] *See id.* at 127 (arguing that "while a non-party state is not itself bound to accept an assertion of jurisdiction over itself unless it has consented, the same is not true of its nationals if they commit offenses in the territory of a state that is a party").

[23] This was the operational theory providing jurisdiction at the Nuremberg tribunals. *See* M. Cherif Bassiouni, *Universal Jurisdiction for International Crimes: Historical Perspectives and Contemporary Practice,* 42 VA. J. INT'L L. 81, 91-92 (2001)(positing that sovereignty does not limit the exercise of criminal jurisdiction to single states)(citing IMT Judgment, Sept. 30, 1946, that signatory states to the London Charter "have done together what anyone of them might have done singly; for it is not to be doubted that any nation has the right thus to set up special courts to administer law.").

[24] *See* van der Vyver, *supra* note 20, at 18 (describing U.S. position with regard to acceptable regimes as an attempt to secure immunity for U.S. citizens).

[25] See id.

[26] Rome Statute art. 16 (allowing the Security Council to delay any investigation or prosecution indefinitely). The Security Council can also initiate prosecution under Article 13(b).

[27] *See* Lawrence Weschler, *The United States and the ICC, in* THE UNITED STATES AND THE INTERNATIONAL CRIMINAL CoURT 85, 93 (Sarah B. Sewall and Carl Kaysen, eds. 2000) [hereinafter "THE U.S. AND THE ICC].

[28] See id.

[29] U.N. Doc. A/CONF.183/10. The Final Act is separate from the Rome Statute and consists largely of a recitation of the events that led to the convening of the Conference and of the proceedings and decisions at the Conference.

[30] These documents may be found at http://www.un.orgilaw/icc.

[31] Rome Statute art. 34.

[32] Id. art. 4.

[33] *Id.* art. 2. The Preparatory Commission adopted a draft proposed agreement in the fall of 2000, which will require further action by the Assembly of States Parties once the treaty enters into force in July 2002, in order to become finalized. *See* Draft Relationship Agreement between the United Nations and the International Criminal Court, U.N. Doc. PCNICC/2000/WGICC-UN/L.1 (2000), *available at* http://www.un.org/law/icc/ prepcomm/ nov2000/english/ wgicclle.pdf.

[34] Rome Statute art. 15.

[35] *Id.* art. 36(3)(b)(i)-(ii).

[36] *Id.* art. 36(7).

[37] See Matthew A Barrett, Note, Ratify or Reject: Examining the United States' Opposition to the International Criminal Court, 28 GA. J. INT'L & COMP. L. 83, 97 (1999) (citing the Rome Statute, art. 41(2)(a)-(b)).

[38] Rome Statute art. 36.

[39] *Id.* art. 36(5).

[40] *Id.* art. 36(8).

[41] *Id.* art. 46.

[42] *Id.* art. 38.

[43] *Id.* art. 39.

[44] *Id.* art. 57.

[45] *Id.* art. 76.

[46] *Id.* art. 83.

[47] *Id.* art. 84.

[48] *Id.* art. 85.

[49] *Id.* art. 42.

[50] *Id.* art. 53.

[51] *Id.* art. 54.

[52] *Id.* arts. 54 and 87(5).

[53] Developments at the Rome Treaty Conference: Hearings before the Senate Comm. on Foreign Relations, 105th Cong. (1998) (statement of David Scheffer, Ambassador-at-Large for War Crimes Issues). For more detail about the procedure for Prosecutor-initiated investigations, see *infra* text accompanying notes 125 *et seq.*

[54] Rome Statute art. 43.

[55] *Id.* art. 43(6).

[56] *See* Christopher Keith Hall, *The First Five Sessions of the U.N. Preparatory Commission for the International Criminal Court,* 94 AM. J. INT'L L. 773, 783 (2000)(describing initiative on the part of Canada, France, Germany, and the Netherlands to address the issue).

[57] Draft Rule of Procedure and Evidence (RPE) Report of the Preparatory Commission for the International Criminal Court; Addendum: Finalized Draft Text of the Rules of Procedure and Evidence, U.N. Doc. PCNICC/2000/INF/3/Add.1 (2000), *available at* http:// www.iccnow. org/html/un.html [hereinafter Draft RPE].

[58] Draft RPE 22 requires that counsel have "established competence in international or criminal law and procedure, as well as the necessary relevant experience, whether as judge, prosecutor, advocate or in other similar capacity, in criminal proceedings."

[59] *See* Draft RPE 21.

[60] *See* Draft RPE 8.

[61] *See* Rome Statute art. 112. The right to vote may be suspended if a state party falls in arrears of its payments for more than two full years. *Id.* art. 112(8).

[62] *See* Lee A. Casey, *The Case Against the International Criminal Court,* 25 FORDHAM INT'L L.J. 840, 845-46(2002) (arguing that the Assembly of States Parties will be a "congress of ambassadors from different and hostile interests" that can claim "no democratic legitimacy even on a theory of virtual representation").

[63] *See id.* at 844.

[64] *See id.* at 845.

[65] Rome Statute art. 5. The preparatory committee was unable to reach a consensus on a definition for the crime of "aggression."

[66] *Id.* art. 8.

[67] *Id.* arts. 124 and 121.

[68] The ICC's jurisdiction may operate in a similar manner with respect to new crimes added by the Assembly of States Parties under the amendment procedures of the Rome Statute. Amendments to add new crimes or change the definitions of those already covered enter into force only for those states parties which have accepted an amendment one year after the deposit of their instruments of ratification or acceptance. The ICC may not exercise its jurisdiction regarding such a crime when committed by nationals of or on the territory of a state party which has not accepted the amendment. The ICC may assert jurisdiction over such crimes committed on the territory of non-party states (or by their nationals) as soon as the amendment enters into force, providing all of the preconditions for jurisdiction are met. *See* Scheffer, *supra* note 14, at 87.

[69] See Didier Pfirter, The Position of Switzerland with Respect to the ICC Statute and in Particular the Elements of Crimes, 32 CORNELLINT'LL.J. 499, 502 (1999) (describing U.S. proposal and initial resistence to the detailed definition of crimes, which is not standard practice in most legal systems).

[70] *See generally* William K. Lietzau, *Checks and Balances* and *Elements of Proof.' Structural Pillars for the International Criminal Court,* 32 CORNELL INT'L L.J. 477 (1999) (exploring issues surrounding establishment of well-defined elements of crimes).

[71] *See* id. at 487 (noting that the need for effective mechanisms to enforce criminal law against individuals requires precision and specificity rather than ambiguity and nuance).

[72] Convention on the Prevention and Punishment of Genocide, Dec. 9, 1948, 78 U.N.T.S. 277. *See* KRIANSAK KITTICHAISAREE, INTERNATIONAL CRIMINAL LAW 69 (2001) (noting that "mobile" groups, such as professions and political groups, are not covered, despite attempts by some delegates at the Rome Conference to include them). [73] *Id.* art. II. Rome Statute art. 6 lists the following acts: Killing members of the group; Causing serious bodily or mental harm to members of the group;

[73] Deliberately inflicting on the group conditions of life calculated to bring about its physical destruction in whole or in part; Imposing measures

intended to prevent births within the group; Forcibly transferring children of the group to another group.

[74] Genocide Convention Implementation Act of 1987, Pub. L. No. 100-606, 102 Stat. 3045 (codified at 18 V.S.C. §§ 1091-93).

[75] *See* KRIANGSAK KITTICHAISAREE, INTERNATIONAL CRIMINAL LAW 69 (2001) (noting that "mobile" groups, such as professions and political groups, are not covered, despite attempts by some delegates at the Rome Conference to include them).

[76] *See id.* at 70 (noting forcible transfer of children as a possible exception because the ultimate result is the physical destruction of a named type of group).

[77] Prosecutorv. Jean Kambanda, Case No. ICfR-97-23-S, ICFR T. Ch., Sep.4, 1998 (former Prime Minister of Rwanda guilty of genocide for failing to take action to halt ongoing massacres).

[78] Report of the Preparatory Commission for the International Criminal Court, Part II, Finalized draft text of the Elements of Crimes, U.N. Doc. PCNICC/2000/1/Add.2, Nov. 2, 2000 (hereinafter "Draft Elements").

[79] *See* KITTICHAISAREE, *supra* note 75, at 72-73.

[80] *See id.* at 86.

[81] *See* Michael P. Scharf, *Justice Versus Peace, in* THE U.S. AND THE ICC, *supra* note 27, at 179, 185.

[82] Rome Statute art. 7 lists: Murder;   Extermination;   Enslavement; Deportation or forcible transfer of population;   Imprisonment or other severe deprivation of physical liberty in violation of fundamental rules of international law; Torture; Rape, sexual slavery, enforced prostitution, forced pregnancy, enforced sterilization, or any other form of sexual violence of comparable gravity; Persecution against any identifiable group or collectivity on political, racial, national, ethnic, cultural, religious, gender as defined in paragraph 3, or other grounds that are universally recognized as impermissible under international law, in connection with any act referred to in this paragraph or any crime within the jurisdiction of the Court; Enforced disappearance of persons; The crime of apartheid; Other inhumane acts of a similar character intentionally causing great suffering, or serious injury to body or to mental or physical health.

[83] *See* Scharf, *supra* note 81, at 87.

[84] *See* Draft Elements, *supra* note 78, at 9.

[85] *See* KITTICHAISAREE, *supra* note 75, at 92.

[86] *See* Douglass Cassel, *Empowering United States Courts to Hear Crimes Within* the Jurisdiction of the International Court, 35 NEW ENG. L. REV. 421, 429 (2001).

[87] *See id.* n.39 (listing relevant crimes over which V.S. courts have extraterritorial jurisdiction). Additionally, U.S. courts have jurisdiction to try criminal offenses committed by persons employed by or accompanying the armed forces overseas, or ex-service members who committed a crime overseas, if such crime would be punishable by imprisonment for more than one year if it had committed within the territorial jurisdiction of the United States. 18 U.S.C. § 3261.

[88] *See* Terrorism and the Law of War: Trying Terrorists as War Criminals before Military Commissions, CRS Report RL31191(summary description of sources and contents of the international law of war).

[89] J EAN PICTET, HUMANITARIAN LAW AND THE PROTECTION OF WAR VICTIMS 31 (1975) (describing the principle that "belligerents shall not inflict on their adversaries harm out of proportion to the object of warfare, which is to destroy or weaken the military strength of the enemy").

[90] Geneva Convention for the Amelioration of the Condition of the Wounded and Sick in Armed Forces in the Field, opened for signature Aug. 12, 1949, 6 U.S. T. 3114, T.I.A.S. No. 3362, 75 U.N.T.S. 31 (entered into force Oct. 21, 1950); Geneva Convention for the Amelioration of the Condition of Wounded, Sick and Shipwrecked Members of Armed Forces at Sea, opened for signature Aug. 12, 1949,6 U.S.T. 3217, T.I.A.S. No. 3363, 75 U.N.T.S. 85 (entered into force Oct. 21, 1950); Geneva Convention Relative to the Treatment of Prisoners of War, opened for signature Aug. 12, 1949,6 U.S.T. 3316, T.I.A.S. No. 3364,75 U.N.T.S. 135 (entered into force Oct. 21, 1950)[hereinafter "GPW"]; Geneva Convention Relative to the Protection of Civilian Persons in Time of War, opened for signature Aug. 12, 1949, 6 U.S.T. 3516, T.I.A.S. No. 3365, 75 U.N.T.S. 287 (entered into force Oct. 21, 1950) [hereinafter referred to collectively as the "1949 (Conventions" or "Conventions"].

[91] Hague Convention No. IV Respecting the Laws and Customs of War on Land, Oct. 18, 1907,36 Stat. 2277, 205 Consol. T.S. 277.

[92] Rome Statute art. 8(1). Art. 8(2). enumerates the following as war crimes: Willful killing; Torture or inhuman treatment, including biological experiments; Willfully causing great suffering, or serious injury to body or health; Extensive destruction and appropriation of property, not justified by military necessity and carried out unlawfully and wantonly; Compelling a prisoner of war or other protected person to serve in the forces of a hostile

Power; Willfully depriving a prisoner of war or other protected person of the rights of fair and regular trial; Unlawful deportation or transfer or unlawful confinement; (viii) Taking of hostages. Other serious violations of the laws and customs applicable in international armed conflict, within the established framework of international law, namely, any of the following acts: Intentionally directing attacks against the civilian population as such or against individual civilians not taking direct part in hostilities; Intentionally directing attacks against civilian objects, that is, objects which are not military objectives; Intentionally directing attacks against personnel, installations, material, units or vehicles involved in a humanitarian assistance or peacekeeping mission in accordance with the Charter of the United Nations, as long as they are entitled to the protection given to civilians or civilian objects under the international law of armed conflict; Intentionally launching an attack in the knowledge that such attack will cause incidental loss of life or injury to civilians or damage to civilian objects or widespread, long-term and severe damage to the natural environment which would be clearly excessive in relation to the concrete and direct overall military advantage anticipated; Attacking or bombarding, by whatever means, towns, villages, dwellings or buildings which are undefended and which are not military objectives; Killing or wounding a combatant who, having laid down his arms or having no longer means of defense, has surrendered at discretion; Making improper use of a flag of truce, of the flag or of the military insignia and uniform of the enemy or of the United Nations, as well as of the distinctive emblems of the Geneva Conventions, resulting in death or serious personal injury; The transfer, directly or indirectly, by the Occupying Power of parts of its own ... civilian population into the territory it occupies, or the deportation or transfer of all or parts of the population of the occupied territory within or outside this territory; Intentionally directing attacks against buildings dedicated to religion, education, art, science or charitable purposes, historic monuments, hospitals and places where the sick and wounded are collected, provided they are not military objectives; Subjecting persons who are in the power of an adverse party to physical mutilation or to medical or scientific experiments of any kind which are neither justified by the medical, dental or hospital treatment of the person concerned nor carried out in his or her interest, and which cause death to or seriously endanger the health of such person or persons; Killing or wounding treacherously individuals belonging to the hostile nation or army; Declaring that no quarter will be given; Destroying or seizing the enemy's property unless such destruction or seizure be imperatively demanded by the necessities of war; Declaring abolished, suspended or inadmissible in a court of law the rights and actions of the nationals of the hostile party; Compelling the nationals of the hostile party to take part in the operations of war directed against their own country, even if they were in the belligerent's service before the commencement of the war; Pillaging a town or place, even when taken by assault; Employing poison or poisoned weapons; Employing asphyxiating, poisonous or other gases, and all analogous liquids, materials or devices; Employing bullets which expand or flatten easily in the human body, such as bullets with a hard envelope which does not entirely cover the core or is pierced with incisions; Employing weapons, projectiles and material and methods of warfare which are of a nature to cause superfluous injury or unnecessary suffering or which are inherently indiscriminate in violation of the international law of armed conflict, provided that such weapons, projectiles and material and methods of warfare are the subject of a comprehensive prohibition and are included in an annex to this Statute, by an amendment in accordance with the relevant provisions set forth in articles 121 and 123; Committing outrages upon personal dignity, in particular humiliating and degrading treatment; Committing rape, sexual slavery, enforced prostitution, forced pregnancy, as defined in article/, paragraph 2(f), enforced sterilization, or any other form of sexual violence also constituting a grave breach of the Geneva Conventions; Utilizing the presence of a civilian or other protected person to render certain points, areas or military forces immune from military operations; Intentionally directing attacks against buildings, material, medical units and transport, and personnel using the distinctive emblems of the Geneva Conventions in conformity with international law; Intentionally using starvation of civilians as a method of warfare by depriving them of objects indispensable to their survival, including willfully impeding relief supplies as provided for under the Geneva Conventions; Conscripting or enlisting children under the age of fifteen years into the national armed forces or using them to participate actively in hostilities. In the case of an armed conflict not of an international character, serious violations of article 3 common to the four Geneva Conventions of 12 August 1949, namely, any of the following acts committed against persons taking no active part in the hostilities, including members of armed forces who have laid down their arms and those placed hors de combat by sickness, wounds, detention or any other cause: Violence to life and person, in particular murder of all kinds, mutilation, cruel treatment and torture; Committing outrages upon personal dignity, in particular humiliating and degrading treatment; Taking of hostages; The passing of sentences and the carrying out of executions without previous judgment pronounced by a regularly constituted court, affording all judicial guarantees which are generally recognized as indispensable. Paragraph 2(c) applies to armed conflicts not of an international character and thus does not apply to situations of internal disturbances and tensions, such as riots, isolated and sporadic acts of violence or other acts of a similar nature. Other serious violations of the laws and customs applicable in armed conflicts not of an international character, within the established framework of international law, namely, any of the following acts: Intentionally directing attacks against the civilian population as such or against individual civilians not taking direct part in hostilities; Intentionally directing attacks against buildings, material, medical units and transport, and personnel using the distinctive emblems of the Geneva Conventions in conformity with international law; Intentionally directing attacks against personnel, installations, material, units or vehicles involved in a humanitarian assistance or peacekeeping mission in accordance with the Charter of the United Nations, as long as they are entitled to the protection given to civilians or civilian objects under the law of armed conflict; Intentionally directing attacks against buildings dedicated to religion, education, art, science or charitable purposes, historic monuments, hospitals and places where the sick and wounded are collected, provided they are not military objectives; Pillaging a town or place, even when taken by assault; (vi) Committing rape, sexual slavery, enforced prostitution, forced pregnancy, as defined in article 7, paragraph 2 (f), enforced sterilization, and any other form of sexual violence also constituting a serious violation of article 3 common to the four Geneva Conventions; Conscripting or enlisting children under the age of fifteen years into armed forces or groups or using them to participate actively in hostilities; Ordering the displacement of the civilian population for reasons related to the conflict, unless the security of the civilians involved or imperative military reasons so demand; Killing or wounding treacherously a combatant adversary; Declaring that no quarter will be given; Subjecting persons who are in the power of another party to the conflict to physical mutilation or to medical or scientific experiments of any kind which are neither justified by the medical, dental or hospital treatment of the person concerned nor carried out in his or her interest, and which cause death to or seriously endanger the health of such person or persons; Destroying or seizing the property of an adversary unless such destruction or seizure be imperatively demanded by the necessities of the conflict; Paragraph 2(e) applies to armed conflicts not of an international character and thus does not apply to situations of internal disturbances and tensions, such as riots, isolated and sporadic acts of violence or other acts of a similar nature. It applies to armed conflicts that take place in the territory of a State when there is protracted armed conflict between governmental authorities and organized armed groups or between such groups.

[93] *See* Draft Elements, *supra* note 78, at 18.

[94] Rome Statute art. 8(1)([The ICC has jurisdiction over war crimes] *"in particular* when committed as a part of a plan or policy or as part of a large-scale commission of such crimes."(emphasis added)). According to the Draft Elements, "elements for war crimes under . . . [the Rome] Statute shall be interpreted within the established framework of the international law of armed conflict " *See* Draft Elements, *supra* note 78, at 18. International law does not appear to require proof of the existence of any policy, official or unofficial, to commit a war crime. *See* Kriangsak Kittichaisaree, *The NATO Military Action and the Potential Impact of the International Criminal Court,* 4 SING. J. INT'L & COMP. L. 498,517 (2000). The "in particular" language is meant to serve as a jurisdictional threshold to prevent the ICC from taking up relatively insignificant cases. *See id.* Critics have argued, however, that this threshold is still too low, increasing the likelihood of prosecution of members of the armed forces. See Jimmy Gurule, United States Opposition to the 1998 Rome Statute Establishing an International Criminal Court: *Is the Court's Jurisdiction Truly Complementary to National Criminal Jurisdictions?*, 35 CORNELL INT'LL.J.1, 30-31 (2002).

[95] 18 U.S.C. § 2441.

[96] Article 18 of the UCMJ, 10 U.S.C. § 818, provides general court martial jurisdiction over "any person who by the law of war is subject to trial by a military tribunal and may adjudge any punishment permitted by the law of war." UCMJ art. 21,10 U.S.C. § 821, provides that court-martial jurisdiction does not deprive military commissions of jurisdiction to try any person for such crimes.   ˙

[97] *See* Department of the Army, FM 27-10, THE LAW OF LAND WARFARE para. 507 (1956).

[98] See generally Silvia A. Fernandez de Gurmendi, The Working Group on Aggression at the Preparatory Commission for the International Criminal Court, 25 FORDHAM INT'L L.J. 589 (2002).

[99] *See id.* at 592 (discussing World War II precedents for charging persons with aggression).

[100] *See* Gurule, *supra* note 94, at 2.

[101] U.N. Charter art. 39.

[102] *See* Kittichaisaree, *supra* note 94, at 504.

[103] U.N. GAOR, Supp. No. 19, U.N. Doc *A/9615* (1974).

[104] *See* Kitticbaisaree, *supra* note 94, at 505 (citing U.N. Security Council Resolution 418 of 4 Nov. 1977).

[105] *See id.* at 504-05.

[106] Rome Statute art. 5(2).

[107] *See* Kittichaisaree, *supra* note 94, at 506 (predicting that "NATO members who are also Permanent Members of the Security Council would certainly veto any draft Security Council Resolution determining that an act of aggression has been committed by NATO").

[108] *See* Scheffer, *supra* note 14, at 83 (advocating U.S. involvement in the ICC to avoid a "definition of "aggression" that does not include a determination by the U.N. Security Council).

[109] The Geneva Conventions require signatory nations to enact domestic legislation to punish perpetrators of grave breaches of the Conventions, and to actively investigate such crimes, and prosecute or extradite the alleged perpetrators. *See* GPW, *supra* note 90, art. 129. Other treaties with similar clauses include the Conventions on Hijacking and Aircraft Sabotage, as well as most other conventions against terrorism. *See* Michael P. Scharf, *Universal Jurisdiction: Myths, Realities, and Prospects: Application of Treaty-based Universal Jurisdiction to Nationals of Non-Party Status,* 35 NEW ENG.L. REV. 363 (2001). *But see* Casey, *supra* note 62, at 855 (disputing the validity of universal jurisdiction). For an in- depth analysis on the applicability of universal jurisdiction to various crimes under international law, see generally Bassiouni, *supra* note 23.

[110] This concept is distinct from domestic jurisdiction. For example, although there is universal jurisdiction over grave breaches of the Geneva Conventions, U.S. law only allows prosecution of such crimes in its federal courts where the victim or perpetrator is a U.S. national. *See generally* Cassel, *supra* note 86 (recommending changes in U.S. law to fully encompass crimes over which the ICC will have jurisdiction); 18 U.S.C. § 2441 (War Crimes Act).

[111] *See* Bassiouni, *supra* note 23, at 136 (concluding that state practice does not support the assertion that universal jurisdiction has reached the level of customary international law in all cases where it has been claimed).

[112] Rome Statute preamble (declaring signatory states are "[d]etermined to put an end to impunity for the perpetrators of these crimes and thus to contribute to the prevention of such crimes").

[113] *Id.* ("Recalling that it is the duty of every State to exercise its criminal jurisdiction over those responsible for international crimes"); *see* Jordan Faust, *The Reach of ICC Jurisdiction Over Non-Signatory Nationals,* 33 VAND. J. TRANSNAT'L L. 1, 7 (2000) (describing ICC jurisdiction as a "form of limited universal jurisdiction").

[114] Rome Statute art. 17. *See* van der Vyver, *supra* note 20, at 2-3 (describing principle of complementarity and the possible questions it raises regarding state sovereignty in any determination of "unwillingness to prosecute").

[115] Rome Statute art. 13 states that the U.N. Security Council may recommend investigation of alleged crimes using its authority under chapter VII of the U.N. Charter.

[116] *Id.* art.16.

[117] *Id.* art. 14.

[118] Draft RPE 45.

[119] Rome Statute art. 14(2).

[120] *Id.* art. 18(1).

[121] *Id.* art. 18(2-5).

[122] *Id.* art. 53.

[123] Draft RPE 107.

[124] Rome Statute arts. 15 and 53(4).

[125] Draft RPE 46.

[126] Rome Statute art. 18(1).

[127] *Id.* art. 15(6).

[128] Draft RPE 109.

[129] U.N. Charter art. 39. *See* Gurule, *supra* note 94, at 22 (criticizing Rome Statute art. 16 for perceived weaknesses).

[130] Rome Statute art. 13(b).

[131] See Mark A. Summers, A Fresh Look at the Jurisdictional Provisions of the Statute of the International Criminal Court: the Case for Scrapping the Treaty, 20 WIS. INT'L L.J. 57,75 (2001); Michael P. Scharf, The United States and the International Criminal Court: A Recommendation for the Bush Administration, & ISLA J INT'L & COMP. L. 385, 387 (2002).

[132] Rome Statute art. 13.

[133] The Rome Statute makes military commanders criminally responsible for the acts of forces under "his or her effective command and control." It also eliminates all immunities "based on official capacity." *Id.* arts. 28 and 27, respectively.

[134] *Id.* art. 13. The concurrence of the state in which the crime took place would be necessary for the ICC to maintain its jurisdiction. The ICC can also

exercise its jurisdiction pursuant to a referral from the Security Council, whether or not the state of nationality or territoriality concurs. Because the U.S. possesses a veto in the Security Council, such a referral could only occur if the U.S. consented.

[135] Such country would also have the option of trying the case in its own courts or extraditing the prisoner to the United States. The Rome Statute provides that states parties who receive a request for surrender from the ICC and a :request for extradition from a non-party state, with which it has an extradition treaty or the like, shall decide which course to take based on the dates of the requests, the interest of the requesting state in prosecuting the crime, and the possibility of subsequent surrender of the person between the ICC and the non-party state. Rome Statute art. 19. If there is no obligation to extradite, the requested state should give priority to the ICC. *Id.* Under Article 98 of the Rome Statute, the ICC may not proceed with a request for surrender or assistance which would require the requested state to act inconsistently with its obligations under international law regarding state or diplomatic immunity or an agreement not to surrender the country's national to the ICC unless the ICC gains the cooperation of that third state. It is unclear whether a treaty violation that results in the ICC's custody of an accused is grounds for challenging the ICC's jurisdiction, either by the accused or the state of nationality of the accused.

[136] *See* Rome Statute art. 17. Paragraph 1 provides the ICC shall determine a case is inadmissible where: The case is being investigated or prosecuted by a State which has jurisdiction over it, unless the State is unwilling or unable genuinely to carry out the investigation or prosecution; The case has been investigated by a State which has jurisdiction over it and the State has decided not to prosecute the person concerned, unless the decision resulted from the unwillingness or inability of the State genuinely to prosecute; The person concerned has already been tried for conduct which is the subject of the complaint, and a trial by the Court is not permitted under article 20, paragraph 3; The case is not of sufficient gravity to justify further action by the Court.

[137] *Id.* art. 20.

[138] *Id.* art. 18. A state has one month after receipt of the notification to advise the ICC that it is investigating (or has investigated) the situation. The Prosecutor must then defer, unless he or she obtains an authorization to investigate from a Pre-Trial Chamber.

[139] Presumably this language refers to both the state where a crime allegedly occurred and the state whose national allegedly perpetrated it, even though

the acceptance of only one of them is *required* for the ICC to find jurisdiction.

[140] *See* Finalized Draft Text of the Elements of Crimes, Report of the Preparatory Commission for the International Criminal Court, PCNICC/2000/1 (2000), *available at* http://www.un.org /law/icc/statute/ elements/elemfra.htm. As currently defined, genocide crimes have as an element that the "conduct took place in the context of a manifest pattern of similar conduct directed against [the target] group or was conduct that could itself effect such destruction." Crimes against humanity include the elements that the conduct was committed with knowledge or intent that it contribute to a "widespread or systematic attack directed against a civilian population." *See id.* at 9. War Crimes listed under paragraphs (a) and (b) of Article 8 of the Rome Statute apply to situations of international armed conflict and incorporate the Geneva Conventions of 1949. Paragraph 2(e) applies to armed conflicts not of an international character and explicitly excludes "internal disturbances and tensions, such as riots, isolated and sporadic acts of violence or other acts of a similar nature." There must be "protracted armed conflict between governmental authorities and organized armed groups or between such groups" before any conduct can be considered a war crime under that paragraph.

[141] Rome Statute art. 12. *See* Ruth Wedgwood, *The Constitution and the FCC in* THE U.S. AND THE ICC, *supra* note 27, at 119, 127.

[142] *See id.* at 127.

[143] *See* Cassel, *supra* note 86, at 437; Robinson O. Everett, American Service members and the ICC, in THE US AND THE ICC, *supra* note 27, at 137, 142.

[144] Rome Statute art. 12(2(c». *See* Gurule, *Supra* note 94, at 27-28 (arguing that the ICC's jurisdiction is not truly complementary because the Rome Statute allows the ICC to second- guess the decisions of national courts).

[145] *See generally* Michael P. Scharf, *Justice versus Peace, in* THE U.S. AND THE ICC, *supra* note 27, at 179.

[146] See, e.g., The International Criminal Court: Hearing before the House Comm. on International Relations, 1O6th Cong. 92-101, 96 (2000) (statement of Monroe Leigh on behalf of the American Bar Association); Scheffer, supra note 14, at 94; Wedgwood, supra note 141, at 123.

[147] See, e.g. Casey, supra note 62.

[148] See generally Robert Christensen, Getting to Peace by Reconciling Notions of Justice: The Importance of Considering Discrepancies Between Civil and

Common Legal Systems in the Formation of the International Criminal Court, 6 UCLA J INT'LL. & FOREIGN AFF. 391 (2001).

[149] Draft RPE, *supra* note 57.

[150] For a brief comparison of ICC procedural safeguards to federal and military rules of procedure and evidence in chart form, see Selected Procedural Safeguards in Federal, Military, and International Courts, CRS Report RL31262. Of course, just as the U.S. Constitution is interpreted in large measure through case law, the Rome Statute may be expected to acquire some new contours in the light of the ICC' s interpretation of the Statute as well as case law interpretation.

[151] See id; Wedgwood, et al., supra note 8, at 130.

[152] *See* Casey, *supra* note 62, at 861-62.

[153] *See* Wedgwood, *supra* note 141, at 1~6 (citing *Ex parte* Quirin, 317 U.S. 1 (1942)).

[154] *See* Madsen v. Kinsella, 343 U.S. 341 (1952)(upholding jurisdiction of military commission to try civilians in occupied foreign territory).

[155] *See* Wedgwood, *supra* note 141, at 122 (giving as an example the International Criminal Tribunal for the Former Yugoslavia).

[156] *See id.* at 124 (citing Charleton v. Kelly, 229 U.S. 447 (1913)).

[157] Rome Statute art. 66.

[158] *Id.*

[159] *Id.* art. 61.

[160] *Id.* art. 61(6).

[161] *Id.* art. 64(8).

[162] *Id.* art. 65.

[163] *Id.* art. 65(3).

[164] *Id.* art. 65(5).

[165] SeeHolbrookv. Flynn, 475 U.S. 560 (1986). A similar rule applies to courts-martial. *See* Manual for Courts Martial (M.C.M.), established as Exec. Order No. 12473,49 Fed. Reg 17,152, (Apr. 23, 1984). Rules for Courts-Martial (R.C.M.) Rule. 804 provides that "[t]he accused shall be properly attired in uniform with grade insignia and any decorations to which entitled. Physical restraint shall not be imposed unless prescribed by the military judge."

[166] Draft RPE 121

[167] Rome Statute art. 54.

[168] *Id.* art. 55.

[169] *See* Wedgwood, *supra* note 141, at 123.

[170] Rome Statute art. 67(1)(g).

[171] *Id.*

[172] *Id.* art. 93(2); Draft RPE 74.

[173] Draft RPE 74.

[174] *Id.*

[175] Rome Statute art. 67(1)(e).

[176] *Id.* art. 68.

[177] Measures to protect national security could also conflict with the accused's right to confront witnesses. *See infra* section addressing the right to a public trial.

[178] Draft RPE 67.

[179] *See* Fed. R. Evid. chapter. VIII.

[180] *See* Maryland v. Craig, 497 U.S. 836 (1990).

[181] See id.

[182] *See id.* at 855 (distinguishing Coy v. Iowa, 487 U.S. 1012 (1988), in which similar measures were invalidated because they were imposed statutorily without requiring a case- specific inquiry into the need for protective measures).

[183] Rome Statute art. 68.

[184] Rome Statute art. 20 *(He his in idem).* "No person who has been tried by another court . . . shall be tried by the Court with respect to the sake conduct unless the proceedings in the other court [were not properly conducted]."

[185] *See* United States v. Lanza, 260 U.S. 377 (1922).

[186] *See* Christensen, *supra* note 148, at 420.

[187] *Id.* art. 20(2).

[188] See Mark C. Fleming, Appellate Review in the International Criminal Tribunals, 37TEX. INT'LL.J. 111, 117(2002).

[189] United States v. Martin Linen Supply Co., 430 U.S. 564 (1977).

[190] Rome Statute art. 81(1).

[191] See id. art. 69(7): Evidence obtained by means of a violation of this Statute or internationally recognized human rights shall not be admissible if: The violation casts substantial doubt on the reliability of the evidence; or The admission of the evidence would be antithetical to and would seriously damage the integrity of the proceedings. See generally George E. Edwards, International Human Rights Law Challenges to the New International Criminal Court: The Search and Seizure Right to Privacy 26YALE J.INT'LL. 323 (2001).

[192] Rome Statute art. 21; Draft RPE 63(5).

[193] G.A. Res. 217A (Ill), art. 12, U.N. Doc. *N810* (1948).

[194] International Covenant on Civil and Political Rights, Dec. 16, 1966, art. 17,999 U.N.T.S. 171,6 I.L.M. 368 (entered into force Mar. 23,1976).

[195] *See* Edwards, *supra* note 191, at 330.

[196] For example, evidence resulting from overseas searches of American property by foreign officials may be admissible unless foreign police conduct shocks judicial conscience or participation by V.S. agents is so substantial as to render the action that of the United States. *See* United States v. Barona, 56 P.3d 1087 (9th Cir. 1995).

[197] Rome Statute arts. 63, 67(1)(d).

[198] Rome Statute art. 63(2).

[199] Illinois v. Allen, 397 U.S. 337 (1970).

[200] Diaz v. United States, 223 V.S. 442,455 (1912).

[201] Rome Statute art. 67(1)(d).

[202] Rule 22 provides: counsel for the defence shall have established competence in international or criminal law and procedure, as well as the necessary relevant experience, whether as judge, prosecutor, advocate or in other similar capacity, in criminal proceedings. A counsel for the defence shall have an excellent knowledge of and be fluent in at least one of the working languages of the Court. Counsel for the defence may be assisted by other persons, including professors of law, with relevant expertise.

[203] Rule 21.

[204] Rule 20 provides that the Registrar "shall organize the staff of the Registry in a manner that promotes the rights of the defence, consistent with the principle of fair trial as defined in the Statute."

[205] Rome Statute art. 67(l)(b).

[206] Fed. R. Evid. 501.

[207] U.S. CONST. Amend. VI.

[208] Rome Statute art. 67(1).

[209] 18 U.S.C. § 3161.

[210] Rules for Courts-Martial (R.C.M.) §707

[211] Strunk v. United States, 412 U.S. 434 (1973).

[212] *See* Barker v. Wingo, 407 U.S. 514, 532 (1972).

[213] *See id.;* United States v. Baker, 63 P.3d 1478, 1497 (9th Cir. 1995).

[214] Draft RPE 84.

[215] Rome Statute art. 29.

[216] 18 U.S.C. §1091(e).

[217] 18 U.S.C. §3281.

[218] 18 U.S.C. §2441.

[219] 18 U.S.C. §3286(b).

[220] 18 U.S.C. §3282.

[221] *See* Waller v. Georgia, 467 U.S. 39, 48 (1984).

[222] R.C.M. §806.

[223] *See* Richmond Newspapers v. Virginia, 448 U.S. 555 (1980).

[224] Rome Statute art. 67(7). 22SDraft RPE 87.

[225] *Id.*

[226] *Id.*

[227] Rome Statute art. 68(6).

[228] Rome Statute art. 87.

[229] *See* Casey, *supra* note 62, at 87 (arguing that the Appeals Division will have identical institutional interests t6 those of the trial chambers and would not be capable of providing truly independent review).

[230] *See* Fleming, *supra* note 188, at 112.

[231] *See, e.g.,* Hirota v. MacArthur, 338 U.S. 197 (1948) (declining to review decision of internationally composed military commission).

[232] *See generally* Fleming, *supra* note 188.

[233] *See Ex parte* Burford, 7 U.S. (3 Cr.) 448 (1806).

[234] *See* Ker v. Illinois, 119 U.S. 436 (1886).

[235] *See* Wong Sun v. United States, 371 U.S. 471 (1963).

[236] Rome Statute arts. 55(lb), 55(ld).

[237] *Id.* arts. 59(3), 60(2).

[238] *Id.* art. 58.

[239] Draft RPE 117.

[240] *Id.* art. 59.

[241] *Id.* art. 59(4).

[242] Draft RPE 117.

[243] Draft RPE 119. Such conditions may include: The person must not travel beyond territorial limits set by the Pre-Trial Chamber without the explicit agreement of the Chamber; The person must not go to certain places or associate with certain persons as specified by the Pre-Trial Chamber; The person must not contact directly or indirectly victims or witnesses; (d) The person must not engage in certain professional activities; The person must reside at a particular address as specified by the Pre-Trial Chamber; The person must respond when summoned by an authority or qualified person designated by the Pre-Trial Chamber; The person must post bond or provide real or personal security or surety, for which the amount and the schedule and mode of payment shall be determined by the Pre-Trial Chamber; (h) The person must supply the Registrar with all identity documents, particularly his or her passport.

[244] Rome Statute art. 60.

[245] *Id.* art. 85; Draft RPE 173-75.

[246] Rome Statute art. 108.

[247] Id. art. 103.

[248] *Id.* arts. 104 and 106.

[249] *See* Scheffer, *supra* note 14, at 74.

[250] *See id.* at 63.

[251] Rome Statute art. 123.

[252] *Id.* arts. 112 and 123. States which have signed the Statute or the Final Act are eligible to participate *as* observers in both bodies. The Administration's notification of intent not to ratify the Statute should have no effect on eligibility, although it may signal an intent not to participate.

[253] U.N. Doc., PCNICC/2001/1/ Add.4, Draft Rules of Procedure of the Assembly of States Parties Jan. 8 (2002) (hereinafter "Draft Assembly Rules").

[254] The United Nations has a standing invitation to participate as an observer. Draft Assembly Rule 35. It may also propose items *for* the agenda. Draft Assembly Rule 11.

[255] Rome Statute art. 13. Non-parties might also be able to provide information to enable the Prosecutor to initiate a self-referred investigation, but would have no *official* role in advocating prosecution.

[256] *Id.* art. 16.

[257] *Id.* art. 53.

[258] *Id.* arts. 86, 87, and 93.

[259] *Id.* arts. 59 and 89.

[260] *Id.* art. 72.

[261] *Id..* art. 73.

[262] *Id.* art. 115.

[263] See Casey, *supra* note 62, at 849-50.

[264] *See* Final Report to the Prosecutor by the Committee Established to Review the NATO Bombing Campaign Against the Federal Republic of Yugoslavia, *available at* http://www.un.org/icty/pressreal/natoO61300.html.

[265] *See* Grossman, *supra* note 6. However, some predict that once the ICC begins to operate, future *ad hoc* tribunals are not likely to be created, which may effectively limit the means available to support such an effort.

[266] The International Criminal Court: Hearing Before the House Committee on International Relations, 106th Cong. 4 (2000) (prepared testimony of John Bolton, Senior Vice President, American Enterprise Institute).

[267] See Appendix I - the French Solution to Constitutional Issues in the International Criminal Court: Manual for the Ratification and Implementation of the Rome Statute at the Canadian government's website on the ICC (http://209.217.98.79/english/l0_guide_e /10_guide_e.htm).

[268] *See* Scheffer, *supra* note 14, at 73 n.94.

[269] *See* Department of Defense Appropriations for 2002, P .L. 107-117. § 8173. None of the funds made available in division A of this Act may be used to provide support or other assistance to the International Criminal Court or to any criminal investigation or other prosecutorial activity of the International Criminal Court. *See also* Departments of Commerce, Justice, and State, the Judiciary, and Related Agencies Appropriations Act, 2002 § 630, P.L.107-77.

[270] H.R. 4546 § 1034.

[271] *See* Grossman, *supra* note 6.

[272] The International Criminal Court: Protecting American Servicemen and Officials from the Threat of International Prosecution, Hearing before the Senate Comm. on Foreign Relations, 106th Cong. (2000).

[273] P.L.I07-117 § 8173. *See supra* note 269.

[274] Rome Statute art. 98 prohibits the ICC from pursuing requests for assistance or surrender that would require the requested state to act inconsistently with its international obligations.

[275] "Covered allied persons" includes military personnel, elected or appointed officials, and other persons working for a NATO country or a major non-NATO ally, which includes Australia, Egypt, Israel, Japan, Jordan, Argentina, the Republic of Korea, and New Zealand, or Taiwan, "so long as that government is not a party to the International Criminal Court and wishes its officials and other persons working on its behalf to be exempted from the jurisdiction of the [ICC]." Sec. 642(3). Coveted allies currently could include persons from the Czech Republic, Turkey, Australia, Egypt, Israel, Japan, the Republic of Korea, and Taiwan. (Of these countries, only Turkey, Taiwan, and Japan have not signed the Rome Statute.) 276H;R. 4775 § 2011; *see also* S. 1610 § 11.

INDEX

D

E

F

G

J

K

L

M

N

O

Q

R

T

Y

Z